INSIGHT POCKET GUIDE

P9-BYJ-050

aTHens

Discovery CHANNEL

APA PUBLICATIONS   **L**
Part of the Langenscheidt Publishing Group

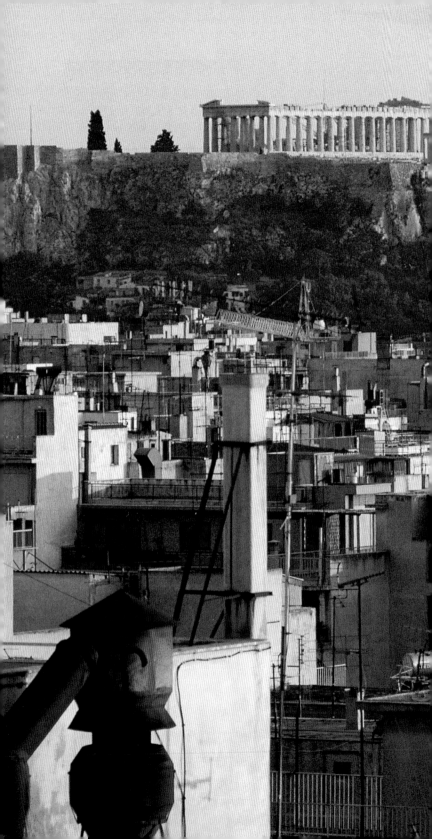

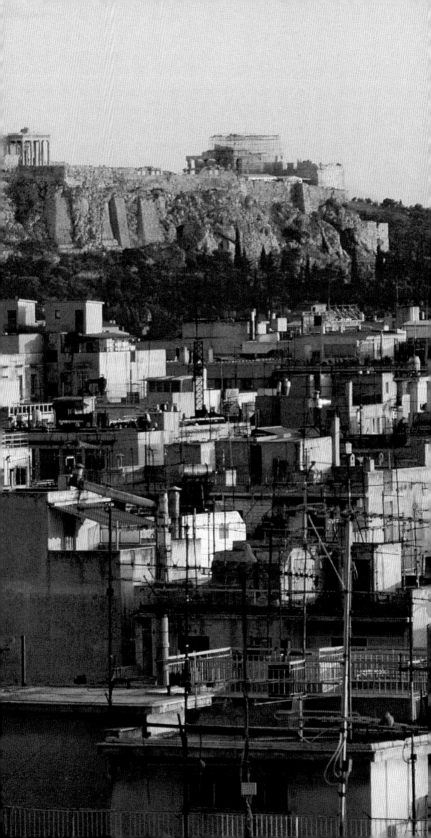

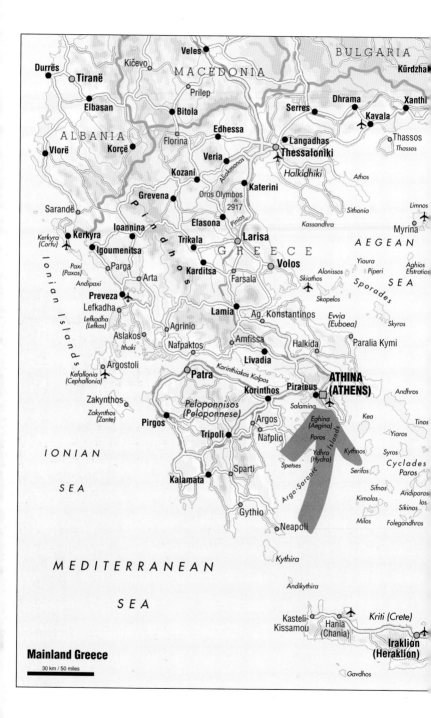

Mainland Greece

30 km / 50 miles

introduction

Welcome

This guidebook combines the interests and enthusiasms of two of the world's best-known information providers: Insight Guides, who have set the standard for visual travel guides since 1970, and Discovery Channel, the world's premier source of non-fiction television programming. Its aim is to help visitors get the most out of Athens during a short stay.

To this end, Insight Guides' expert on Athens, Elizabeth Boleman-Herring, has devised a series of itineraries. The first three have been designed as full-day tours devoted to the must-see attractions of the city and its surroundings – the Acropolis and other ancient sites, the island of Aegina, and the historical centre – while the remaining 14 tours highlight other interesting areas and aspects of the city. As a contrast to the city's hustle and bustle, excursions are included to ancient Delphi and Corinth and to the island of Hydra. Following the itineraries are ideas on eating out, shopping and nightlife, and a wealth of practical tips.

Athens is well worth the undivided attention it gets in this guide. It is the magnet towards which all Greeks – and all things Greek – gravitate. It is a city that first burns itself on the senses, and then, given half a chance, on the heart. No marble but Athenian marble smells so pungent after a fall of rain. No coffee tastes better than that brewed off Omonia Square. No conversations sound as intense as those overheard in the Zappeion.

 Elizabeth Boleman-Herring lived in Athens for over three decades after being taken there by her father in 1961. She says of the city: 'Athens is an addiction I resisted as a child, but have succumbed to as an adult. Here the rare, quintessentially Greek things, the things that really matter, seem to remain the same. The capital may be smoggy, deafening in certain districts and plagued with inefficiency, but the swallows still return to nest in Athens' sooty rafters each spring, the Parthenon still sparkles like Aphrodite on her half-shell and the Saints' Day festivals ensure at least one feast of faith and fun per month.'

HISTORY & CULTURE

From the powerful city-state of ancient Athens, in which philosophy flourished, to the hectic metropolis of today – a concise history of Greece's illustrious capital **11**

ATHENS & ENVIRONS

These guided tours concentrate on the must-see sights. Stops for refreshment are suggested in each itinerary.

Preceding Pages: the Acropolis
Following Pages: modern Athenians

Ο ΔΟΣ
ΛΥΣΙΚΡΑΤΟ
LYSIKRAT

History
& Culture

There are four hills on the Athenian skyline. In addition to the limestone platform of the Acropolis, with its crown of 5th-century BC temples, there is the Hill of the Muses, which is topped by the Roman-era Philopappou Monument; Mount Likavitos (Lycabettus), with its tiny, white-washed Chapel of St George; and, farthest north, the rocky spine of the Tourkovounia ('Turkish mountains').

Each hill in the vast smoggy bowl of concrete that comprises the modern Greek capital, the city the Greeks call *Athína*, bears testimony to Athens' unbroken history. Inhabited since the Neolithic period, Athens is a settlement some 8,000 years old. From a mere campfire on the spring-fed Acropolis ('high city'), the site has become an unruly megalopolis, lapping up to Mount Parnitha (Parnes) to the northwest, Mount Pendeli to the north, and spilling past violet-hued Mount Imitos (Hymettus) to the east. The smog generated by Athens-based industry and traffic cannot escape this ring of mountains, and the constant noise of motorbikes, lorries and cars ricochets off the city's concrete walls.

Well over a third of Greece's population – some 3.8 million people – now lives in the capital, and it is becoming increasingly hard to locate a 'real' born-and-bred Athenian among the immigrants from the Pelopónnisos (Peloponnese), the islands, Asia Minor, Egypt, Turkey, the Philippines, the Sudan, the former Yugoslavia and all the stations of the Greek diaspora abroad. (Recent newspaper headlines proclaimed that one in 10 'Greek' workers is now foreign-born, with Albanians, Pakistanis, Filipinos and Iraqis predominating: 1,500,000, residents of Athens alone are foreign-born.)

Increasingly, the Athens we see is not the Athens we come to see, and end up seeing. It's what's up there on the hills above the smog, and in the museums, that draws us. The Athens we come to see is the Ghost of Athens Past, the Athens of Pericles and Phidias. The fact is that Athens shone most brightly in the 5th and 4th centuries BC, and has been resting on its laurels ever since. In the space of some 200 years the city produced, in one miraculous sunburst, the likes of Aeschylus, Aristophanes, Aristotle, Diogenes, Euripides and Socrates.

Neither before nor since has there been such an eruption of intellect, excellence and creativity in one small space, in one brief period of time, and it is no exaggeration to say that, due to the city of Athens, we in the West are what we are, think what we think, perceive as we perceive. Western civilisation's entire cultural heritage is mirrored in those vestiges of Periclean Athens preserved on the modern city's skyline: we all live in the shadow of the Parthenon.

Left: the 5th century BC Temple of Hephaistos (aka The Theseion)
Right: classic profile

First and Foremost, Ionians

It didn't all happen overnight, of course. In fact, two mighty civilisations, the Cretan Minoan and the Mycenaean, rose and fell before Athens came to dominate the Greek scene, a relative latecomer. Athens had to invent a myth wherein a native son, Theseus, son of King Aegeus, outwitted Minos of Knossos. By solving the problem of the labyrinth, with the help of the Cretan king's daughter, Theseus was able to put to an end his city's subservience to the southern island-kingdom. He slew the dread Minotaur, and no more would Athens be required to send its nine-yearly 'luncheon' of seven maids and seven youths to the half-bull/half-man in the maze.

In reality, Minoan civilisation had ended centuries before the Athenians felt the need to brush up on their own (lack of) early history. Indeed, civilisation in general in Greece ended before the rise of Athens. In the 12th century BC, the Dorians swept down from the north and blotted out the palaces of Mycenae, and all that they implied. Life became brutish and short for some 300 years during the Greek 'Dark Ages'. The Athenians alone, of the original Ionian stock in the south, weathered the storm, their Greek culture intact.

Fast forward to the 9th century BC, perhaps earlier in enlightened Athens, and civilisation begins to flicker back on again. The alphabet (from *alpha, beta*, of course) was adopted in Greece, a dramatically different pottery painting style, the Protogeometric, was devised and, in Ionia, the Homeric epics were composed.

In the 7th century BC, Greece was divided into *polises*, or city-states, whose inhabitants – the subjects of kings, for the most part – shared a language, worshipped the same pantheon of Olympian deities, celebrated the Olympic

To Megálo Horió (The Big Village)

If one considers that the population of the capital has tripled since World War II, with immigrants pouring in from Greece's devastated and impoverished towns, it is no wonder Athens is often called 'the big village'. Village mores and customs are still alive and well in the metropolis. Grandmothers dressed in perpetual mourning spit on their chests three times to ward off the Evil Eye; offices are exorcised against The Eye as well; drivers leave vans stranded in the middle of the street (like the donkey of yore) while they rush into a shop to collect something; and dowries, though illegal, are still paid out to bridegrooms. For some, the veneer of Coach or Hermès briefcases and Diesel T-shirts is just

that – a veneer. Beneath the surface, Athenians are for the most part village Greeks at heart, still holding sacred the taboos and traditions passed down for centuries by the Church, and Church fathers, and the pseudo-religious folk-laws the Church never quite stamped out. Swinging from your cab driver's rear-view mirror may well be an icon of the Virgin of Tinos, placed there by his wife to protect him from mayhem on the road. His little fingernails may have been allowed to grow to half an inch in length to demonstrate that he is no longer a man of the fields. And the worrybeads in his hand? Another artefact not quite at home in a big city, and considered the height of gauche by Athens' young professionals.

Above: an 'early owl' Attica drachma

Games together and held a distinctively Greek world view. Athens, the capital of Attica, was moving towards a more democratic form of government, however, and this set it apart from its more conservative fellow *polises*.

Athens' hereditary kings gave way to hereditary archons, who were in turn replaced in the late 9th century BC by a nine-member oligarchy. Draco codified the Athenian laws in 621BC, and Solon enacted sweeping reforms – cancelling land debts and freeing slaves, establishing representative assemblies – foreshadowing Pericles' enlightened rule of a century later.

Blueprint for Democracy

A spate of coups followed, carried out by *tyrants*, dictators who seized power, but Solon had sketched out an almost indelible blueprint, and the design would suffice until Pericles could build on it, following decisive wars with the East. The Persian Wars of 490 to 479BC were a turning point in Greek as well as world history. If Darius had conquered Athens, the West would not have been. As it was, however, the Persians were defeated, first at Marathon, and then at Salamis. Xerxes, son of Darius, met his match in the Athenian fleet, which was used to defend the Athenians when they fled their city for the safer Saronic Gulf islands.

Athens was destroyed by the Medes, but the naval victory against their stronger Persian foe inspired the returning citizens to rebuild their city and erect a temple dedicated to their goddess-protector, Athena. From 479 until 431BC, democracy flourished and the city-state became a major power in the then-known world. The Delian League was established, its treasury paying for Pericles' ambitious building schemes, and Piraeus (Pireás) was fortified.

Power struggles among the city-states preceded the so-called Peloponnesian Wars of 431 to 404BC (actually, between Athens and Sparta). Concurrent with this conflict, plague broke out in Athens, claiming the life of Pericles in 429BC, and Athenian society divided into two embattled groups: those supporting the oligarchy, and those advocating democracy. The oligarchs won out, briefly, during the second round of hostilities with the neo-Dorian Spartans, but democracy was restored following an Athenian victory. It was a short-lived restoration: Athens fell to Sparta in 404BC, and was never again to be a great power.

In the 4th century BC, Athens, Thebes and Sparta vied for supremacy, with Persia behind the scenes, tipping the scales when one of the three became too powerful. In 399 BC, Socrates, in one of Athens' saddest hours, was condemned to death in the Agora for 'corrupting the morals' of Athenian youth. In 387BC, Socrates'

Right: pillars of the Parthenon

disciple, Plato, founded his Academy; his own follower, Aristotle, would go on to tutor Alexander the Great, son of Philip of Macedonia.

In the mid-4th century BC, Philip engineered a war against Athens and Thebes and defeated the two city-states, whereupon he established the League of Corinth. His plans for this nascent league of little nations were aborted due to his assassination in 337BC, when the reins of power passed to Alexander, whose love for Athens protected the city from harm during his lifetime.

Town and Gown

The Hellenistic Age saw Athens' democracy again replaced by an oligarchy in the wake of Alexander's death in 323BC. Athens was now well on its way to becoming a university town, a role it would play for the next 850 years. Plato's Academy, Aristotle's Lyceum, Zeno's stoicism, Epicurus' epicureanism – these were the magnets that attracted visitors to Athens during the Hellenistic period. Rome to the west, a great admirer of all things Greek, did not much trust the Hellenistic kings, however. But while the Greek colonies, Macedonia, Corinth and Piraeus felt the sword of Rome, the ghost of Periclean Athens brought out the best in the conquerors from the Tiber. The Romans came to Athens bearing gifts. They erected the monuments at Eleusis, the Roman Library and Agora, completed the Temple of Olympian Zeus, and Hadrian constructed a water-conduit on the slopes of Mount Likavitos. Vespasian even installed public latrines near the Tower of the Winds, also a Roman gift, and once a working water-clock. Herod Atticus, another Roman patron of Athens, raised the theatre where today's Athens Festival events are staged, as well as the Athenian Stadium, later restored by Ziller for the 1896 Olympiad. However, in AD267, the Herulians, originally Scandinavians, invaded the city, taking up where the Dorians had left off.

Above: 1825 icon, *Blind Eros and The Sirens*

This was the beginning of the end for Rome, and for Roman Athens. An earlier, and all but unnoticed visitor to the Acropolis and the Areopagus, where he addressed the assembled Athenians, was one Paul, formerly of Tarsus, and though Christianity was slow to take hold in Greece, Paul's religion would transform the country as surely as had Pericles' new ideas about government. In AD529, the Emperor Justinian dealt 'Classical Athens' its death blow by closing down forever the 'pagan' schools of philosophy. In the 5th century AD, Iktinos' and Phidias' Parthenon was converted into a Christian church. Yet if the light of the 5th century had gone out in Athens, the torch was passed to the Athens of the East, Constantinople.

An Unlikely Capital

Athens slept through the following 1,000 years and control of the city passed from Franks to Turks to Venetians. During the period of Turkish rule, the Parthenon served as a mosque for the Turkish garrison billeted atop the Acropolis. During one Venetian bombardment in 1687, the Parthenon, along with the Turkish munitions dump housed there, suffered a direct hit.

Another desecration was the Seventh Earl of Elgin's removal of precious marbles from the Acropolis and the Parthenon proper in 1799. Phidias' frieze and metopes now reside in the British Museum, a subject of much debate in modern Athens. In 1829, when the Turks left Greece following their defeat during Greece's War of Independence, Athens was no more than a potent idea held sacred by the European powers determining Modern Greece's history. The first capital of the nascent state was Náfplio (Nauplion), in the Pelopónnisos; the seedy village of Athens was subsequently chosen as the site for the nation's capital by virtue of its past splendour. First offered to Prince Leopold of Saxe-Coburg, who accepted and then changed his mind, the 'throne' of King Aegeus was then offered to Otto, the 17-year-old son of King Louis I of Bavaria. Athens was no more than a hamlet of some 6,000 people, but something of the spirit of Pericles remained, defiant, in the hearts of the populace: when the Bavarian king refused to grant his subjects some of the rights due to them, they forced him to abdicate.

Over the next century-and-a-half, Athens came slowly to dominate the economic and political life of the country. By far the largest city of the modern state, it still draws migrants from the depopulating Greek countryside, and while this makes the city vibrant, bustling and endlessly fascinating, the pressures on housing, health care and transport and communications infrastructures continue to challenge the city's administration.

Right: the teenage King Otto of Bavaria

HISTORICAL HIGHLIGHTS

BC

Circa 6000 First Stone-Age settlement on the Acropolis.

683 Collapse of the kings. Power is then distributed amongst the Athenian nobility.

490 The Battle of Marathon. Athens under Themistocles defeats Darius' Persian army.

480 The Persians, under Xerxes, over-run Attica and lay waste to Athens. The population flees to Salamis, where Themistocles mounts a successful naval counterattack. The Temple of Aphaia is built on Aegina.

478 Piraeus becomes an important commercial centre; the Delian League is formed to replenish the treasury after the war with Persia.

461 The Dawning of Athens' so-called Golden Age. Pericles becomes head of state and Athens flourishes until his death in 429.

440 The Temple of Poseidon is completed at Sounion.

438 Phidias completes work on the Parthenon.

431 The Peloponnesian War – the city of Sparta refuses to recognise Athens' pre-eminence. After years of plague, Athens is defeated and the Peloponnesian War finally ends in 404.

322 Athens is occupied by the Macedonians, but is left unharmed due to the esteem in which Alexander the Great holds the city.

146 Rome destroys Corinth and occupies Greece.

86 After Athens supports Mithridates of Pontus, the Roman general Sulla attacks the city and Piraeus is destroyed. Athens loses all political significance – Corinth becomes the capital – but retains its cultural influence.

AD

50 St Paul visits Athens and preaches on the Aereopagus.

117 The Emperor Hadrian pays his first visit to Athens. He begins construction of the Temple of Olympian Zeus (completed in 138), and extends the city significantly, building the gate which still bears his name.

150 Herod Atticus of Marathon becomes patron of the city and builds the theatre which bears his name beneath the Acropolis.

267 During the Emperor Valerian's protectorate the Goths, led by the Heruli, invade and pillage Athens, but are driven out by the Romans.

330 Constantinople becomes the capital of the Byzantine Empire, many of its treasures having been removed from Athens.

395 The Olympic Games are banned by Theodosius II as being heathen.

529 The Emperor Justinian closes Athens' university and the city's philosophical schools.

1456 Turkish forces succeed in taking Athens, having previously conquered Constantinople.

1687 26 September: a direct hit by a Venetian cannonball on a Turkish powder magazine damages the Parthenon.

1799 Britain's Lord Elgin removes the Parthenon Marbles.

1821–31 Greek War of Independence.

1832 Otto of Bavaria becomes ruler of Greece after France, Britain and Russia declare the country a kingdom in 1831.

1834 Athens, a town of 6,000 people, is declared the capital.

1838 The Royal Palace (now the Parliament) is completed on Syntagma (Constitution) Square.

1863 George I, a former prince of Denmark, becomes king after Otto's deposition.

1896 The first modern Olympiad.

1910 Eleftherios Venizelos becomes Prime Minister.

1912–13 The Balkan Wars.

1913 George I is assassinated in Thessaloniki, and is succeeded by Constantine and his wife Sophia.

1916 With Venizelos declaring for the entente and Constantine practising neutrality due to German sympathies, Greece is split in two; Venizelos then forms a provisional government in Thessaloniki.

1917 Constantine flees to Switzerland, leaving his son Alexander in charge. Venizelos returns to Athens.

1919–22 'The Great Idea' leads to the disastrous Greco-Turkish War; 1.5 million refugees return to Greece. Between 1920 and 1928, the population of Athens doubles.

1920 King Alexander dies after being bitten by a pet monkey.

1922 After the war against the Turks, Constantine is deposed by a military coup; his son becomes George II. Venizelos represents Greece in peace negotiations with Turkey.

1923 George II is deposed; a republic is declared.

1935 The monarchy is restored and George II reinstated.

1936 George II supports the dictatorship of General Metaxas. Venizelos dies in Paris.

1940 The Italians invade Greece.

1941 German troops enter Athens, but the Greeks' spirited defence costs Hitler two months.

1941–2 Under the Germans, 300,000 Greeks die of famine.

1944 12 October: British troops arrive in Athens. 18 October: George Papandreou, Prime Minister in exile, returns. December: left-wing uprising suppressed by government backed by British troops.

1946 Civil war breaks out. Elections held. Royalists win a majority after a communist boycott.

1947 United States military aid granted to Royalists. Paul I becomes king.

1949 Civil war ends. Hundreds of thousands are dead and millions displaced, having sought safety in major cities.

1950–66 Constantine Karamanlis becomes Prime Minister in 1956, to be defeated by Papandreou in 1964.

1967 Constantine II, son of Paul I, goes into exile after a military coup; 'The Colonels' take power.

1973 A protest at Athens Polytechnic is crushed with bullets and tanks.

1974 With Greece on the brink of war with Turkey, the dictatorship ends and the people vote for a republic, deposing King Constantine, and returning Karamanlis as premier.

1980 After paving the way for entry to the European Economic Community, Karamanlis is defeated in elections by Andreas Papandreou.

1981 Greece joins the EEC.

1989 Papandreou is implicated in a major economic scandal but is later acquitted. Two elections bring hung governments.

1990 Third election narrowly won by New Democracy. Constantine Mitsotakis becomes Prime Minister. Karamanlis is elected president.

1993 Antonis Samaras, former New Democracy Foreign Minister, creates new party, 'Political Spring'. At elections Papandreou's PASOK returns to power. Miltiades Evert becomes leader of New Democracy.

1995 Constantine Stephanopoulos is elected President.

1996 Kostas Simitis takes over as Prime Minister.

1999 Earthquake kills 143 in Athens.

2002 Greece adopts the euro; Dora Bakoyianni elected Mayor of Athens.

2004 In January, Simitis cedes PASOK party power to Foreign Minister George Papandreou. In general elections held in March PASOK is defeated by the New Democracy party, led by Costas Karamanlis, ending 23 years of socialist rule. From 13–29 August Athens hosts the Olympic Games.

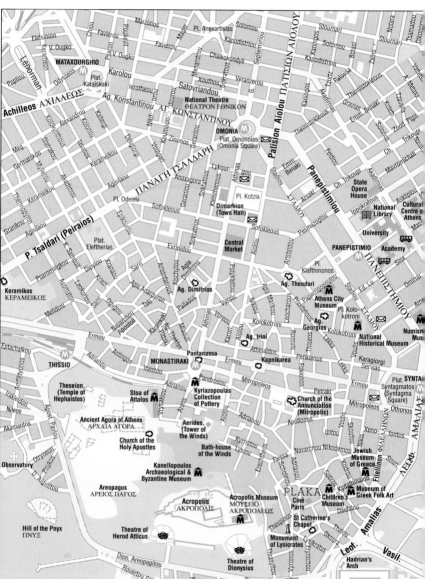

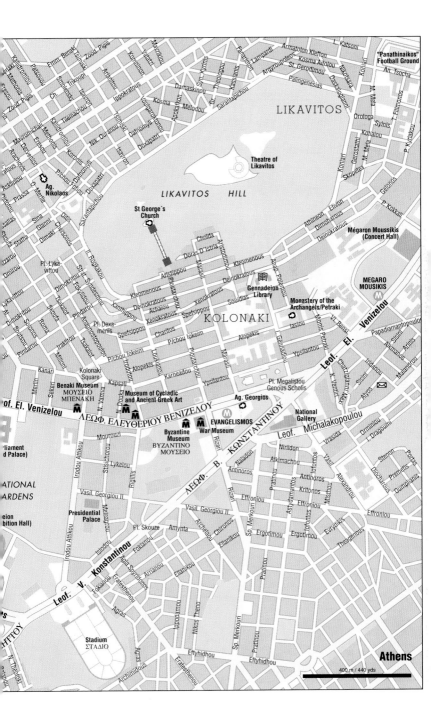

Athens

400 m / 440 yds

City
Itineraries

V isiting Athens requires energy and, in high season, patience. Visitors can usually deal with the smog, the erratic opening hours and the heat, but to avoid the queues and crowds, get up bright and early, preferably on a Sunday, to scale the city's 'marble' heights.

1: ATHENS' MARBLE HEART *(see map, p23)*

Have Greek coffee at Dionysos; hike up to the Acropolis for a tour of the temples and the Acropolis Museum; stroll through the Ancient Agora; browse in Monastiraki; sample *ouzo* and nibbles or coffee at The Beautiful Greece café; detour to the Tower of the Winds; witness the changing of the guard; dine at Orizondes Likavitou or the Aigli Bistro.

Wear sensible shoes and take sun block, sunglasses and hat, and carry bottled water (which is pricey on the site).

Before embarking on this route, you may want to reserve a table at **Orizondes Likavitou** (restaurant) or the **Aigli Bistro** the day before, for 7.30 the following evening. Try also to arrange tickets for Athens Festival performance (June–Sept) or at Athens' new concert hall/opera house, the Mégaron Moussikís, for a concert, opera or recital (although these usually need to be booked well in advance).

There are two 'approaches' to the **Acropolis** and its temples (daily Mar–Oct 8am–7pm, Nov–Feb 8am–5pm; tel: 210 323-6665; 321-4172 for holiday closings and free admission days. Retain your ticket, as it is good for a week's entry to antiquities included in the six 'Unification of Archaeological Sites'), and both have their proponents. The first school of thought holds that visitors must spend at least a day doing their homework so they can tell the metopes from the pediments up there; the second advocates picking up a copy of Manolis Andronicos' *The Acropolis,* on sale at the café gift shop across from the site, to do some quick thumbing before taking off up the hill. Both groups will find a visit to the Parthenon and other structures on the rock rewarding.

In summer, the earlier you start out the more time you will have before the sun turns the city centre into a frying pan. The best way to get to the Acropolis is from the new Akropoli metro station on Makryianni Street. The previously traffic-filled Dionysiou Areopagitou Street has now been pedestrianised, making it a pleasant stroll to where the path winds up to the entrance gate of the archaeological site. The **Dionysos Café** (on Rov. Galli Street near the roundabout beneath the

Left: the Parthenon, Athens' most famous sight
Right: the Erechtheion's caryatid-columns (detail)

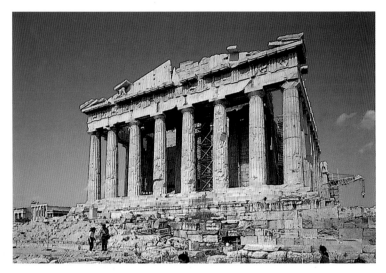

Acropolis on Dion. Areopagitou) opens at 8am, and it is a good place to sit for a while over a Greek coffee and look up at the imposing east side of the Acropolis. Visible from here are the Propylaia, the Temple of Athena Nike, the brow of the Parthenon proper and, at the foot of the rock, the Roman-built, 2nd-century AD Theatre of Herod Atticus, where Athens Festival performances are staged in summer. (Near here as well is the site of a projected new Acropolis Museum, conceived of as a home for the Parthenon Marbles now in London's British Museum.)

Beulé Gate

It's a 10-minute walk from the Dionysos Café to the **Beulé Gate**, uphill on a slick stone walkway which will prepare you for the treacherous surfaces

ahead. Watch your step. (Of course, in antiquity, these marble surfaces were covered with soil and landscaped.)

The area on top of the rock is described in a clockwise direction. First of all you pass up through the Beulé Gate and the Propylaia – the monumental 5th-century BC gatehouse which cost almost as much to build as the Parthenon itself. On the right, look for the exquisite **Temple of Athena Nike** (or 'Victorious' – hence the famous brand of sportswear).

The next obvious sight is the Erechtheion, built on the most ancient site on the Acropolis, with its porch held aloft by the caryatids, statues of graceful young women supporting the entablature with their heads (the ones here are cement copies: most of the originals are in the museum).

Above: the magnificent facade of the Parthenon
Left: the Beulé Gate

Carry on, around the Parthenon to the **Acropolis Museum** (opening hours are those of the Acropolis proper) on the southeastern corner of the site. Your entrance fee to the Acropolis also covers the museum, which is cool and contains what Lord Elgin did not manage to cart off to Britain. Though an international debate now rages about whether or not the British Museum should return the Parthenon Marbles to the structure of which they are an integral part, one priceless artifact is forever lost. The Parthenon sculptor Phidias's towering gold and ivory statue of Athena (26 cubits tall, according to Pliny) had vanished by the time fire ravaged the Parthenon in the 3rd century AD, long before European predators descended upon Greece's treasures.

Ancient Agora

Coming down again through the Beulé Gate, bear right following signs to the Ancient Agora. An outcrop of stone on your left, with a bronze plaque set into the rock beneath it, is the **Areopagus**, or Rock of Ares, the war god, where in AD50 St Paul spoke to the assembled Athenians about 'the Unknown God' (Acts 17:22–34). His words were persuasive enough to convert one Senator Dionysius, who later became Dionysius the Areopagite, patron saint of Athens. The view is worth the scramble up. The chapel-topped cone in the distance is Mount Likavitos, which you may be seeing at close hand later.

Turn left into the **Ancient Agora** (daily May–Oct 8am–7pm, Nov–Apr 8am–5pm; museum closes 30 mins before the site; tel: 210 321-0185; admission charge, but free to holders of a 'Unification' ticket), strolling through precious 5th-century BC rubble to the wire gate and entrance booth. Inside the gate, pass the late 10th-century Church of the Holy Apostles and ramble down to the Stoa of Attalos, now the **Stoa of Attalos Museum**.

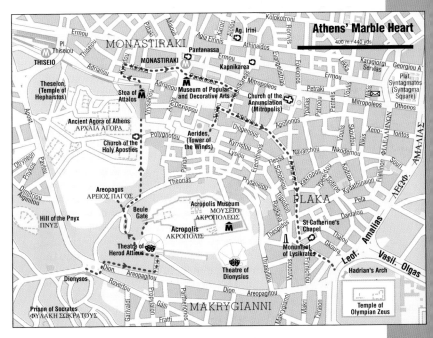

The largely intact Doric hexastyle **Temple of Hephaistos**, also known as the Theseion, is to the northeast of the site.

This first itinerary may be rather long for some visitors, and those with more time may like to split it in two at this point – skipping to dinner at Orizondes Likavitou or the Aigli Bistro (see *page 25 for details*) before resuming the route the next day.

Flea Market

For those who wish to carry on with the tour, exit the Agora into Adrianou Street at tiny **Avissinias Square**, where a number of street traders spread out their piebald wares near St Philip's Church daily from 9am–2pm (Sun and holidays, 9am–1.30pm) and on Sunday mornings there is live music. From here turn right into Adrianou Street, proceed half a block and go right on Kynetou, then turn immediately right again on Ifaistou, which is named after the god of the forge (Hephaistos, husband of Aphrodite).

You are now in the bustling heart of Athens' Flea Market, the confusingly named **Monastiraki**, or Little Monastery area. Ifestou empties into Monastiraki Square, where the Church of the Pantanassa (the Little Monastery), the Mosque of Tzistarakis and what still remains of the great Library of Hadrian, can all be found.

Bear right towards the mosque on the corner of Areos Street and the square, cross Areos and enter Pandrosou Street. At No. 89, you will find Stavros Melissinos, the 'poet sandalmaker', whose excellent sandals and books of poetry are a charming bargain, purchased either separately or as a package. (This is the man who apparently made sandals for John Lennon.) A little further up the street, at No. 50, you will come across the fine and reliable **Martinos Antiques** which, along with **Martha Kapsoulakis'** shop at No. 36, has a license to trade in antiquities.

At No. 36 Pandrossou (and 59 Mitropoleos streets) is the **Centre of Hellenic Tradition**, with its varied selection of traditional Greek crafts, all reasonably priced. Upstairs, after browsing, you may like to sip an early watered *ouzo* and eat a platter of Greek hors d'oeuvres *(pikilía)*, or try a Greek 'spoon sweet' *(glykó koutalioú)* a sort of marmalade over yoghurt: nice with Greek coffee.

Turn right off Pandrossou onto Aiolou Street for a detour up to the **Tower of the Winds** (8.30am–3pm, admission charge), a 1st-century BC sundial, weather vane and water-clock on the edge of the Roman Agora (used by dervishes, during the period of Turkish rule, as a place to perform their whirling dances). Backtrack on Aiolou to Adrianou Street, and follow this at a snail's pace through the old city of Athens, or **Plaka**, till it empties into a little square on which there is a sunken chapel, St Catherine's. If the building is open, go in and have a look around this church, which was granted to the Monastery of Mount Sinai in the late 18th century. Exit the square onto Lysikratus Street which leads onto Amalias Avenue at the **Temple of Olympian Zeus** (daily 8am–3pm; tel: 210 922-6330; admission charge, but free to holders of a 'Unification' ticket).

Left: funerary monument to Philopappus

Fine Food and Views

If you've reserved a 7.30pm table at Orizondes Likavitou or the Aigli Bistro, try to be in front of the **Parliament** building on Syntagma Square just before 7pm (the exit from the Syntagma metro station will bring you out just across the road from the Parliament). On the hour, you will see the changing of the *évzone* guard, an elite group of crack troops decked out on Sundays and holidays in the traditional *foustanélla* – white, pleated kiltlette – worn by mountain fighters during the Greek War of Independence (1821–31).

To get to the restaurant, take the metro from Syntagma to Evangelismos. If you're fit, walk uphill on Ploutarchou Street, which will lead you, in about 10 abbreviated vertical blocks, to the entrance to the **Likavitos** *teleferique*, or funicular tramway. (The funicular runs every 30 mins, 9am–3am daily.) If you have had enough hiking for the day, it's best to make this ascent by taxi from the Evangelismos metro station. Orizondes Likavitou is a new, pricey eclectic-Greek restaurant atop **Likavitos**: the views are spectacular, north, south, east and west, and the Athenians are grateful they finally have grand cuisine atop their city's 'other' grand rock.

The **Aigli Bistro** features another sort of ambience: fine, if expensive, Greek cuisine enjoyed al fresco in the magnificent **Zappeion Gardens**. From Syntagma metro station, walk south on Amalias Avenue and turn left into the gardens opposite St Paul's Church. Walk approximately ¼ mile (½ km) east, passing the Zappeion Mansion. The restaurant is next door to the mansion.

In the evening, you may proceed from dinner to: 1) a performance of theatre, music or ballet at **Herod Atticus Theatre**, just underneath the Acropolis; 2) a performance of **Dora Stratou Greek Dances** at the troupe's refurbished theatre on Filopappou Hill; or 3) off season, between October and April, a performance at the superb new **Concert Hall** *(Mégaron Moussikís)*, corner of Vasilisis Sofias Avenue and Kokkali Street, which attracts international orchestras and soloists. *See page 72 for details on how to book.*

Above: an evening of dance

2: AEGINA – THE 'ISLAND SUBURB' *(see pull-out map)*

The early hydrofoil to Aegina; Temple of Apollo and Aegina Museum; Temple of Aphaia; bus to Perdika and water taxi to Moni islet for a swim; lunch at a fish taverna; optional overnight extension at a traditional guest-mansion, taking in a performance at Ancient Epidaurus Theatre.

Take snorkelling gear if you plan to swim, a beach towel, a sweater for the island evening and something casual but smart for Epidaurus or dinner at Mikrolimano.

Between June and September, the **Ancient Theatre at Epidaurus** hosts a festival of Ancient Greek drama, and one of the most pleasant ways to attend a play is via the Saronic Gulf island of Aegina. If you do arrive in high season and are interested in attending a play, plan to spend at least a night on Aegina at the **Aiginitiko Archontiko** (Ag. Nikolaou & Thomaïdou 1; 18010 Aegina; tel: 22970-24968; when you book, tell the owner, Fotis Voulgarakis, that you want to see a play as well as stay the night). If you arrive in Athens off season, a night on Aegina without the Epidaurus side trip is also a pleasant change from Athens' smog and bustle. The island has just about everything: sun, sea, fresh fish, its own roasted pistachios, a gorgeous sanctuary, nightlife and more.

Flying Dolphin

Phone the hydrofoil company the night before you set out for Aegina to enquire about the early morning hydrofoil, or Flying Dolphin departures: Hellas Flying Dolphins, tel: 210 419-9200; or Saronic Dolphins, tel: 210 422-4777. The hydrofoils for Aegina leave from Piraeus' Agios Spyridonas harbour and you should catch the earliest Dolphin out to make the most of your day on the island.

Top: moored in Piraeus
Above: one form of transport in Aegina

athens & environs

The morning of your departure, take an early metro to Piraeus (line 1). The hydrofoils depart from the Agios Spyridonas harbour in Piraeus, about 10 blocks from the Piraeus metro/train station on the Akti Miaouli. It takes about 45 minutes early in the morning to travel from the centre of Athens to the harbour (the hydrofoil departure quay is a 5-minute walk from the metro), so make sure you allow enough time.

The hydrofoil trip from Piraeus to Aegina Town takes about 35 minutes in good weather. If you take the 6am or 7am hydrofoil, you'll arrive before Aegina Town opens up for the day. If you don't have a return ticket, buy your ticket home, either for that same evening or the next day, from the booth on the hydrofoil pier, and then either phone Fotis Voulgarakis at the Aiginitiko Archontiko (he'll collect you and your bag from the port), or take a stroll up the harbourfront and choose a café for coffee and breakfast – the traditional **Aiakeion** is a favourite. After breakfast, pick up a packet of pistachios *(fistíkia)*, Aegina's most famous commodity.

Temple Visits

At this point, you may want to visit the **Temple of Apollo** (8.30am–3pm) – ask for Kolona, a three-minute walk to the northwest end of town – as well as the **Aegina Archaeological Museum** (Tues–Sun 8.30am–3pm; admission charge) and the Temple of Aphaia *(see below)*. Kolona means 'column' in Greek, and that is all that remains in place of the 6th-century BC Temple of Apollo that once stood here. The little museum, however, preserves much more of Aegina's illustrious classical history, though the richest finds now belong to the National Archaeological Museum in Athens and, in the case of the Temple of Aphaia, to the Glypothek in Munich (Ludwig of Bavaria bought the pedimental sculptures in 1811).

On the way back from the Temple of Apollo, in the square just north of the main quay, find the bus terminus and taxi rank. Look out for the bus to Agia Marina, and enquire about departure times. Buy your ticket (inexpensive) before alighting (buses depart every 2 hours and the journey takes around 30 minutes), and get out at the **Temple of Aphaia** (daily 8.15am–7pm; Oct–May closed at 5pm; tel: 22970-32398; admission charge; you may want to check these opening times before making your journey, as they tend to change). The museum is only open by prior appointment (tel: 22970-32398) for 15 minutes at 9am, 11am, 12 noon and 1pm.

After touring this beautifully preserved 5th-century BC sanctuary of the nymph Aphaia, worshipped on Aegina alone since the 2nd millennium BC, you may choose to cross the street and relax over a cold drink at the café/gift shop overlooking the town. The walk down to town (about 3km/2 miles) is pleasant in spring when it isn't too hot, and you can browse in the shops and have a swim or a snack in the resort village of **Agia Marina**.

Right: Temple of Aphaia

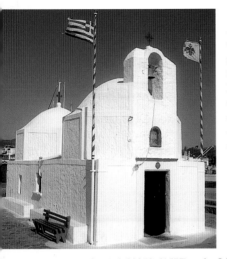

Alternatively, catch the bus back to Aegina Town and take the next bus to the seaside village of **Perdika**, to the south. (The bus journeys to Agia Marina and Perdika take 20–30 minutes.) Perdika is a fishing village with a string of excellent fish tavernas and easy access to the islet of **Moni** and the island of Angistri *(see itinerary 3 below)*, both excellent spots for strong swimmers and snorkellers. The water taxi leaves from the quay for Moni regularly. The trip takes 10 minutes, and the swimming, in clear, green Aegean water, is best off the rocks to the left of the tiny port.

Arrange your departure from Moni so as to have time for lunch at either Proraion (tel: 22970-61577) or the O Nondas (tel: 22970-61233), the taverna nearest the bus stop. Aegina is noted for its grilled or boiled octopus as well as fish. Take a look at the morning's catch in the kitchen.

If you're planning on going to **Epidaurus** for the evening, allow time for the bus trip back to Aegina Town. If you're returning to Athens, allow time to have coffee on the waterfront before catching the Dolphin. Those not staying the night may in any case want to go and see the Aiginitiko Archontiko, near St Nicholas' Church and the pink Tower of Markellos. Take a walk through the mansion, originally a residence of Ioannis Capodistrias, the first President of Greece, and of Aegina's native-born saint, Nektarios. Built in the 1820s, it features beautiful painted ceilings. The rooms and suites are heated in winter and air-conditioned in summer. Those en route to Athens may want to pick up pistachios and Aegina honey at Zoes Dionysios near the hydrofoil pier. Sweet tooth? Sample the cakes at the harbourfront **Aiakeion Café**.

If you arrive in Piraeus and did not get your fill of fish on Aegina, you may want to hail a cab and proceed to **Mikrolimano**, also known as Tourkolimano, a tiny harbour lined with good fish restaurants near the main Piraeus port. Ask for **Jimmy and The Fish** (46 Akti Koumoundourou, tel: 210 412-4417; €€) or **Plous Podilatou** (42 Akti Koumoundourou, tel: 210 413-7910; €€): the former, for simple seafood; the latter, for creative Santorinian fare.

3: THE ISLET OF ANGISTRI *(see pull-out map)*

A day-trip to, or overnight or extended stay on Angistri, an islet beyond Aegina in the Argo/Saronic Gulf.

Angistri means 'hook', and hooked you will be.

If the Argo/Saronic Gulf island of Aegina, with its taxi rank and discos, is still not idyllic enough a day-trip from busy, smoggy Athens, be advised: paradise is on the horizon in the form of tiny **Angistri**. Most visitors still get around this pine-covered gem on foot. There are only four 'settlements'

Above: sugar-cube church, Aegina
Right: sea view

of any size (you cannot really call them 'villages'), the entire island is ringed with lovely beaches and coves (there is actually even one nudist beach on Angistri: **Halikiada**), and a few buses plus a handful of taxis supplement the little fleet of mopeds to provide transport.

Pure, Phosphorescent Paradise

Catch the catamaran *E/G Keravnos* instead of the Aegina hydrofoil in Piraeus. It departs from Little Karaiskaki Square and, in fact, stops first at Aegina before continuing on to Angistri. There are morning, midday and evening departures in high season. Tickets are very reasonable – purchase them from a booth near the catamaran – and the voyage takes about an hour. A day or so ahead of your trip, phone Mr Leonidas Thanopoulos and Ms Nelly Asimakopoulos, who own and manage the delightful hotel/studios called the **Alkyoni** (18010 Angistri, tel: 22970-91377/8; €€). The hotel is named after the mythical Halcyon bird, which was supposed to possess the power to calm the winds and seas as it rested on the waves at the winter solstice.

Nelly and Leonidas, an Athenian lawyer who fled the pollution and noise of Athens, have created a mini-resort with its own swimming grotto, gorgeous sea views of Aegina and a fabulous in-house restaurant. Everything in nearby **Skala** 'town' is within walking distance, and the sea is alive with fish and other viewing pleasures. Do not miss night swimming amidst Angistri's sparkling, phosphorescent plankton, a rare experience so close to Athens.

Should the Alkyoni be full, call Katerina or Yanna, the helpful duo at **Skala Tours** (Skala, 18010 Angistri, tel: 22970 91502, 91228, 91356, fax: 22970 91342; e-mail: nik.panou@otenet.gr), who can arrange alternative lodging and/or snorkelling tours, visits to dramatic performances at Ancient Epidaurus, tours of nearby Aegina and various cruises.

athens & environs

4: THE INNER CITY HISTORICAL AND ECCLESIASTICAL WALKING TOUR *(see map, p31)*

A morning-into-afternoon 'circle of the squares'; churches and markets; City Hall; Omonia Square and the Neon Café; the National Library, University and Academy; Athens' Cultural Centre and Theatre Museum.

Begin your walking tour in the morning, on the hour, at **Syntagma Square** watching the changing of the guard in front of the Tomb of the Unknown Soldier. Then turn your back on Parliament (the old Royal Palace) and head down Georgiou A Street past the **Hotel Grande Bretagne** (built in 1842–3 as a private family residence). The street changes names at the Stadiou Street lights, becoming Karagiorgi Servias. For those who have missed breakfast, a block down Karagiorgi Servias, take a few steps to the right into Voulis Street and stop at **Ariston**, at No. 10, for the best *tirópitta* (cheese pie) in Athens.

At the end of Voulis Street is the **National Historical Museum** (13 Stadiou Street, tel: 210 323-7617; 322-2266; Tues–Sun 9am–2pm; admission charge; Sun, entrance free; closed Mon), in an imposing 19th-century structure that was the Greek Parliament building until the 1930s. Its holdings – costumes, furnishings, weaponry, ships' figureheads, etc – illustrate the history of the modern Greek state, from the fall of Constantinople in 1453 through the 1940 war between Greece and Italy.

A popular restaurant is located next to the museum, the **Palia Vouli**. Dine al fresco in summer; come back for the piano bar later.

Back on Karagiorgi Servias, proceed another block to Leka Street and turn right. This is the busy heart of the mercantile and publishing city centre. On the left side of the street as you proceed are some of Athens'

Above: Evzones guard the Tomb of the Unknown Soldier
Left: icons on Aiolou Street

most skilled silversmiths: note the silver worrybeads and silver-chased icons.

Cross Kolokotroni Street, where Leka turns into Praxitelous. Continue down Praxitelous and, on the right at No. 30, is **Doris**, where they've been serving *loukoumades* since 1900. Go in, sit down and order some of these hot Greek doughnuts smothered in honey and cinnamon, or perhaps lunch.

Continue for a quarter of a block and on your right, up Skouleniou Street, is the tiny, sunken mid-11th-century **Church of St Theodore** (Agios Theodori). Call in if the church is open. Backtrack on Skouleniou and turn right on Praxitelous. Look up as you walk and you'll see the 1921 mosaic facade at No. 38 Praxitelous. Turn left on Hrissospileotissis Street. Half a block down on your right is the **Church of the Golden Virgin of the Cave**, named after a miraculous icon found on the Acropolis. Circle around to the front of the church and you'll find a kiosk *(períptero)* selling votive offerings and incense. This church celebrates its feast day on 15 August.

Buy Your Own Icon

As you stand facing the church, to your right down the pedestrian walkway you will be able to see the Acropolis in the distance. About two blocks down Aiolou towards the Acropolis, at the Square of St Irene, is a flower market adjoining the graceful **Church of St Irene** (Ag. Irini) Athens' first cathedral. Take a peek inside this beautiful structure before turning right down Agia Irini Street. At No. 8–9, look out for the icon shop **To Ayio Oros** ('The Holy Mountain') where, if you possess a saint's name (Anthony, Catherine, Helen, etc.) you might purchase a painted metal image of your patron or patroness.

A block further down, turn right onto Athinas Street. To your left, you can see **Monastiraki Square** and the **Church of the Pantanassa**, with the **Flea Market** stretching beyond. On Athinas, the whole world seems to be for sale. This is a wonderful area in which to shop for unusual, inexpensive

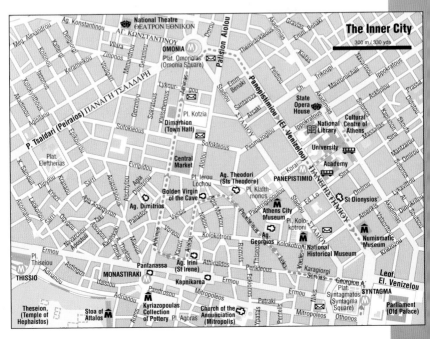

gifts, such as wooden bread stamps, metal icons and brass and copper household items. About four and a half blocks further up Athinas, the congestion intensifies. Pass Evripidou Street, and explore the huge meat and fish markets on your right and the fruit and vegetable markets on your left.

Continue on Athinas Street to **Kotzia Square**. On your left is the Dimarhíon (Town Hall). In the square are the yellow and white National Bank buildings. The Athens Stock Exchange is on nearby Sofokleous Street. Athinas Street empties into **Omonia Square** where the popular Everest pie and sandwich bar occupies the corner site. Now cross Athinas to the left. The square is a centre for fast-food restaurants: should you wish to stop for a coffee and perhaps a slice of walnut cake, **Neon** (No. 8, on the opposite side of the square) is the best. Omonia is full of X-rated kiosks, traffic and gaggles of men talking politics or idling. It's still a bit of a tip even after the metro excavations have been completed, but worth observing. (If you're tired, the Omonia metro station offers a quick route back to Syntagma Square or Plaka.)

As you leave Neon, walk straight ahead and then turn left onto El. Venizelou Street, popularly known as Panepistimiou (University) Avenue. About four blocks down on the left are the National Library, the **University** and Athens' Academy. Have a good look at the porch of the University with its frescoes representing the Arts, Sciences and Greek men of learning. Next to the University, is the gilded and painted Academy. Between the University and the Academy, on its left, is a pedestrian mall (Patriarchou Grigoriou) which connects El. Venizelou with Akadimias Street. Directly ahead of you is the **Cultural Centre of Athens** (50 Akadimias Street, tel: 210 362-1601; 363-0706; daily 9am–1pm, 5–9pm; closed Mon and Sun afternoon), at the head of a circular drive. This building houses the **Museum and Study Centre of Greek Theatre** on its ground floor – well worth a detour.

Cross Sina Street and continue down El. Venizelou past the neo-Byzantine Eye Hospital and St Dionysius' Roman Catholic Cathedral, named after Athens' first Christian convert. Cross Omirou (Homer) and Amerikis streets, and pass the house built between in 1870 and 1881 for Heinrich Schliemann, who unearthed Troy, now the **Numismatic Museum** (12 Panepistimiou Street, tel: 210 823-2534; Tues–Sun 8am–2.30pm).

5: A QUARTET OF MUSEUMS
(see map, p34)

A full itinerary combining four of Kolonaki's excellent museums.

These are some of the best museums in Greece, with exemplary displays and facilities.

Begin at the **Benaki Museum** (Mon, Wed, Fri and Sat 9am–5pm, Thur 9am–midnight, Sun 9am–3pm, closed Tues; tel: 210 367-1000, www.benaki.gr; admission charge), the corner of Koumbari Street and Vasilissis Sofias Avenue, just across from the National Gardens. This fabulous collection was established in 1930 by aristocrat and philanthropist Andonios Benakis, whose heart is immured at the museum's entrance. Recently expanded and renovated, the museum aims to present an unbroken tradition of Greek identity through artefacts from neolithic times to the mid-20th century. The Benaki Museum has an excellent café and gift shop and is a favourite of the Athenian intelligentsia.

Among the most impressive displays are the collections of traditional costumes, mostly bridal and festival dresses, and the reconstructed reception rooms of a mid-18th century Kozani mansion. Also of great interest are the displays of gold on the ground floor, and the collections relating to the Greek struggle for independence.

Afterwards, proceed away from the gardens for two blocks on Vasilissis Sofias, then turn left up Neofitou Douka Street. At No. 4, on your right, is the fascinating and visually stunning contemporary **Museum of Cycladic and Ancient Greek Art** (daily 10am–4pm, Sat 10am–3pm, closed Sun and Tues; tel: 210 722-8321, www.cycladic.gr; admission charge). Many exhibits in this museum are explained by wall posters detailing Cycladic history, everyday life, burial customs, etc. Thus the museum instructs as well as preserves: the high standard of presentation of individual artefacts is unmatched elsewhere in Greece.

The ground floor houses a small, exclusive gift shop with high quality reproductions, books and cards, and there is also a pricey garden café (which moves indoors in winter). The first floor is devoted to Cycladic artefacts; the second floor covers Greek art from 2000BC to the 4th century AD. The third floor houses temporary exhibitions, while the fourth displays artefacts from the 4th century BC to the 6th century AD, as well as fragments of Cycladic figures from the Keros hoard.

Gracious Athenian Living

Included in the ticket is a visit to the magnificent 'Helen Stathatou' neoclassical home, which was built in the last century by the architect Ernst Ziller. Just follow the long signposted corridor from the ground floor.

Left: the main fish market
Above: painting from the Benaki Museum. **Right:** Cycladic figurine

athens & environs

The mansion, which once belonged to one of the city's leading families, has been superbly and tastefully renovated and gives an idea of gracious Athenian living in bygone days. It also gives you a glimpse of what Kolonaki looked like before World War II: a lovely area with elegant homes and gardens free of smog.

Exit from the building on the corner of Vas. Sofias and Irodotou, cross the main avenue and walk half a block towards the Athens Hilton. There you will find the former 'Florentine Renaissance' mansion of the eccentric Duchesse de Plaisance (she who had her beloved, deceased daughter embalmed in alcohol and then died when the bier caught fire). The buildings, ranged around a central courtyard, house the **Byzantine Museum** (daily 8.30am–3pm, closed Mon; tel: 210 721-1027; admission charge).

The collection comprises early Christian works from the 4th to the 7th century AD, art of the Middle Byzantine period, artefacts from the Frankish occupation and Palaiologan period (1204–1453) and, most important, a collection of fine icons. The latter, housed on the second floor of the main building, are worth seeking out even if you are a bit museum-weary by now.

At the corner of Vasilissis Konstantinou and Vasilissis Alexandrou avenues is Athens' **National Gallery** *(Ethnikí Pinakothíki)*, which houses a collection of contemporary Greek art (usually eclipsed by the city's fine private art galleries) but which frequently holds interesting exhibitions (Mon and Wed 9am–3pm, 6–9pm, Thur–Sun 10am–2pm, closed Tues; tel: 210 723-5857; admission charge). The El Grecos are reason enough to visit this collection.

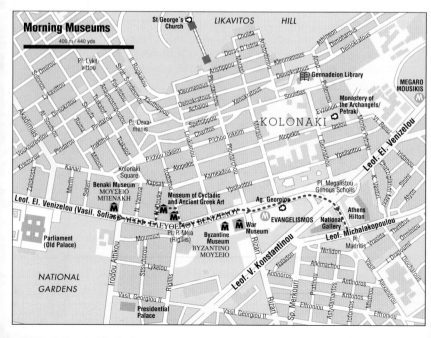

6: PIRAEUS *(see pull-out map)*

An archaeological museum, Sunday flea market and taverna.

Reserve for lunch or dinner at Vasilenas (Mon–Sat) before embarking.

Piraeus, the great port of Athens, is a city in its own right, and merits several visits in order to savour its salty delights. This excursion highlights three of its attractions which may be combined with a Flying Dolphin trip to the Saronic Gulf islands (see *Itinerary 2: Aegina* and *Excursion 1: A Day on Hydra*). If you set out for Piraeus on a Sunday morning, combine a visit to the Archaeological Museum with a tour of the 'Monastiraki of Piraeus', a large flea market on and around Dragatsaniou and Mavromichali streets.

Focusing on the finds of maritime archaeology, the **Archaeological Museum of Piraeus** (31 Harilaou Trikoupi Street, Piraeus, tel: 210 452-1598; Tues–Sun 8.30am–3pm, closed Mon; admission charge) contains statues, reliefs and funerary monuments from Piraeus, western Attica, the Saronic Gulf islands and the island of Kythera. Perhaps the most striking exhibits are the bronzes in Room 3 (first floor). Among these are the Piraeus Apollo, dating from the 6th century BC, and Athena, her helmet graced with owls and griffins (both discovered in Piraeus port in 1959). Also impressive is the mausoleum of an Istrian merchant.

Also worth a look is the **Naval Museum of Greece** (Zeas Marinas, tel: 210 451-6264; Tues–Fri 9am–2pm, Sat 9am–1.30pm, closed Sun and Mon; admission charge) containing model ships, equipment, uniforms, etc, documenting Greek life at sea.

Any day but Sunday, try **Vasilenas** (72 Etolikou Street, Piraeus, tel: 210 461-2457; €€), a taverna noted for the quantity and quality of its food. Ask to see its guest book before you leave: Winston Churchill and Tyrone Power once dined here.

Left: 17th-century icon at the Byzantine Museum
Above: Zea harbour, Piraeus. **Right:** a bronze statue of Athena

7: THE TEMPLE OF POSEIDON *(see pull-out map)*

A day trip to Cape Sounion, visiting the Temple of Poseidon.

To get the most out of this itinerary, get up early and take the metro to the Victoria stop, from where it is a short distance to the Mavromataion bus stop that serves Sounion.

Cape Sounion and the **Temple of Poseidon** (daily 10am–sunset; tel: 22920 39363; admission charge) are a 65-km (40-mile) jaunt down the corniche which runs along Athens' Saronic Gulf. The site is easy to reach by public transport (although some visitors may prefer to take one of the guided tours offered by GO, CHAT or Key Tours).

Buses for Sounion leave regularly from the corner of Mavromataion and Leoforos Alexandras (just by Areos Park; closest Metro station Victoria). Try to catch a bus that drives along the sea past all Athens' Saronic Gulf coast beaches – Faliron, Glifada, Vouliagmeni and Varkiza – rather than inland, as the former is quicker and of more interest. The Sounion stop is close by the sanctuary and return buses run until fairly late (check with KTEL for exact times, tel: 210 823-0179; 821-3203). Buses run from the centre 5.45am–5.30pm, and the one-way journey takes 1½ hours.

The temple dates from the 5th century BC, but the site was occupied as far back as prehistoric times and is mentioned in Homer's *Odyssey*. Unfortunately, due to wear and tear by tourists' shoes and the tendency of visitors to leave their marks (even Byron carved his name on one of Sounion's columns), the temple proper is now roped off and inaccessible to visitors.

The two rows of 16 remaining columns are poised in a magnificent location overlooking the **Saronic Gulf**, and the site is particularly dramatic at sunrise

Above: the Temple of Poseidon, Sounion
Right: sand and sea

or sunset. Archæological sleuths have assigned the Temple of Poseidon to the same architect responsible for designing the Ancient Agora's Hephaisteion. The marble used at Sounion came from Agrileza, about 4km (2½ miles) north of the site. Unlike Pentelic marble, this stone contains no traces of iron, and so has remained a brilliant white. The eastern frieze depicted the battle of the Centaurs, while the sculptures of the eastern pediment probably depicted the competition between Poseidon and Athena for control of Athens. The western side is completely destroyed.

You may opt for a longer stay at Sounion. About 1.5km (1 mile) downhill (4km/2½ miles by the winding, paved road) is the modest hotel **Aegeon** (tel: 22920-39200; €€), on a small, sandy beach. Next door is the **Taverna Akroyiali**, a lovely place for grilled octopus and fish (tel: 22920-39107; €). Swimming off the beach here offers a wonderful view of Poseidon's temple.

8: SWIM ON THE ATHENIAN RIVIERA *(see pull-out map)*

Get away from the city and sample the delights of a private beach.

Make an early start and head out to the beach by Express bus.

In the run-up to the 2004 Olympics, many of the EOT (Greek National Tourist Organisation) beaches of the 'Athenian Riviera' were privatised, resulting in much improved facilities. In addition, ecological measures have been taken to clean up the Saronic Gulf and 'blue flags' (for clean beaches) now abound.

There are many, many beaches on the coast south of Athens, priced to suit every pocket, but two are recommended here.

The family-friendly **Apollonies Aktes** (formerly Voula A Beach) features a broad sandy beach, shallow water and is not far from the city centre. There are sun-beds, a beach bar, open-air events at the Blue Water and Verde venues, plus water slides and a water sports centre. From the Panepistimiou Street bus terminal, across the street from the Athens Academy, take the E2 Express bus (the banner reads 'Akadimia-Voula') and ask for 'Apollonies Aktes'. The trip takes about 1 hour. The beach is open daily in summer 7am–11pm (tel: 210 895-1646; admission charge).

More sophisticated and pricier than Apollonies Aktes is **Asteras Vouliagmenis Beach**, featuring the ruins of a 5th-century BC Temple of Apollo, fine sand, a gently sloping sea, water and beach sports and the possibility of hiring a motorboat for a trip to the islet of **Fleves**. There is fine waterfront dining at Taverna 37 and the Club House.

From the Panepistimiou bus terminal, take bus No. A2 as far as Glyfada Square *(Plateía Glifádas)*; then change to the No. 114 bus: one ticket covers the 1-hour trip. The beach is open 8.30am–6pm in season (tel: 210 890-2000; admission charge).

9: THE KAISARIANI MONASTERY *(see pull-out map)*

Spend three hours or more at a cool, monastic retreat situated on the outskirts of the city.

It is, perhaps, the loveliest place within a stone's throw of the city, so buy ingredients for a picnic lunch and a bottle of red wine (take a corkscrew and glasses), and head for the hills.

One of the best vantage points for viewing the city – at some distance from all its smog and noise – is from a tiny picnic spot at the edge of a pine wood

above the **Monastery of Kaisariani** (tel: 210 723-6619). The perfect place for an al fresco lunch followed by a fresh-air hike in spring, summer or autumn, Kaisariani is also a birdwatchers' and botanists' delight. Five kilometres (3 miles) from Athens' city centre, at a height of 450m (1,475ft) above sea level, the 300-hectare (750-acre) site is the carefully tended property of The Athens Friends of the Trees Society. The site is open Tues–Sun 8.30am–3pm, but is closed on Mon throughout the year.

The trip up to Kaisariani from the Athens Hilton will take under 20 minutes by taxi, and you'll be dropped off at the bottom of a small hill. Ask for the monastery: there's a very reasonable entrance fee, but the gatekeeper will tell you how to make a donation to the Friends of the Trees if you're interested. There is a lovely book on sale in the card shop, *Mount Hymettus and the Kaisariani Monastery*, by Kaity Argyropoulo, which really gives you a feel for the place, both the buildings and the gardens.

The monastery at Kaisariani dates from the 11th century, and the **Church of the Virgin**, and the **Church of St Anthony** nestled against it, are ornamented with exquisite 16th- and 17th-century murals. This is a very special place to visit on 15 August, when the Dormition of the Virgin is celebrated.

After viewing the churches and the adjoining monastery buildings, ask the gatekeeper to direct you to the spring, with its 6th-century marble ram's head, which has been a place of pilgrimage since pagan times. The spring has always been ascribed curative powers, but whether or not one believes that Kaisariani's waters are miraculous – especially for the infertile, it is said – they keep the surrounding gardens well watered, and provide a welcome oasis in the heat of summer.

Again ask the gatekeeper for directions, this time uphill towards the **Church of the Archangels** *(Ee Eklisía ton Taksiárchon)*, and the medieval cemetery of the monks. After a five-minute climb on a dirt path through an

Above: the Kaisariani Monastery
Right: the church at Daphni

olive grove, you will come across the now ruined 10th-century **Church of the Assomaton Taxiarchon**, and the adjacent **Chapel of St Mark Frangomonastiro**. Turn left from these structures, and you will see picnic tables and benches and, beyond, a stunning view of Athens, the Acropolis and the sea. This is the place to open your wine, unpack your lunch and enjoy the pristine air and the birdsong.

After lunch, take the path back down to the monastery, turn left on the paved road, and walk downhill for another 2.5km (1½ miles) to a little roundabout just beneath the Kaisariani cemetery *(Nekrotafíou Kaisarianís)*. Here, city bus No. 223 or 224, which departs every 10 minutes or so, will take you back into the centre of Athens. Watch out for landmarks such as the Athens Hilton, and get off on Vassilissis Sofias Avenue, where you can get on the metro back to your lodgings.

10: THE MONASTERY OF DAPHNI
AND ANCIENT ELEUSIS *(see map, p41)*

Allow 1½ hours in the morning for the Monastery of Daphni; three hours total if you go on to see Eleusis. Pack a lunch for Eleusis, and be warned: it's a hot, exposed site in summer.

Note that, at present, the Monastery of Daphni is undergoing extensive renovation work, and there is no public access to the site. Telephone before visiting, or check with Tourist Information on 210 327-1300-1 or at www.culture.gr to see if it has reopened.

Determined Byzantine culture vultures will not want to miss seeing the 5th-century **Monastery of Daphni** (closed at present; tel: 210 581-1558), with its exquisite 11th- and 12th-century mosaics matched only by those in Ravenna and Istanbul. It nestles in an oasis of Mediterranean pines about halfway between Athens and Eleusis on the **Sacred Way**, a thoroughfare as profane today as it was holy to the Ancient Greeks making their way to the Temple of Demeter at Eleusis to take part in the Eleusinian Mysteries. In fact, the original basilica was erected – incorporating fragments of the

athens & environs

Sanctuary of Daphnaios Apollo, including one graceful Ionian column that escaped Lord Elgin – to tempt the idolatrous en route to Eleusis and win them over to the One True Faith.

Eleftherias Square, also known as Koumoundourou Square, is a short walk down Panagi Tsaldari Street from Omonia Square. Locate the fountain on the square (twin cormorants, or some such bird, spouting water). The buses for Daphni and Elefsina stop by the fountain. Board a No. A16 or B16 bus from Akadimias Street, off the square, and ask the driver or an obliging fellow traveller to tell you when the bus reaches the stop for the monastery *(Moní Dafníou)*. The trip, through uninspiring, working-class neighbourhoods, takes about 20 minutes: the bus is likely to be crowded and you will probably have to stand. (Do not confuse Dafní – the location of the monastery – with Dáfni, which lies at the end of the new red metro line 2; they are on opposite sides of the city.)

Step down outside the Daphni Mental Hospital (bus stop *Psychiatrío*). Retrace your way a little and cross the busy highway. Turn right along the access road (signposted to Daphni Byzantine Monastery). The entrance to the monastery is on your left, about 150 metres/yds down. You may want to pick up Paul Lazarides' useful archaeological guide to the site which, when it reopens, will help you to identify the mosaics in the church and give you an appreciation of the architecture.

Above: the company of men
Left: the dome of Daphni Monastery

Ancient Eleusis

If you came to Athens specifically to see the antiquities, **Ancient Eleusis** (daily 8.30am–3pm, closed Mon; tel: 210 554-6019; admission charge) is worth seeing. It is not located in a beauty spot – the Elefsina petrol refineries, among Greece's largest, are in the immediate neighbourhood – but the temple site is impressive and the small museum lovely.

To get there, back on the other side of the highway, where your Athens bus driver let you off for Daphni, catch the A16 or B16 for Elefsina. Ask the driver or fellow passengers to tell you when you reach the stop for Ancient Eleusis, which is also the stop for the bakery *(foúrno)*.

Cross the highway and proceed down the pedestrian walkway towards a pale blue clock tower, topped by the Greek flag, on a gentle rise (local people will gladly point the way). The clock is actually on the site of Ancient Eleusis, which hasn't been overrun with tourists. Signs will guide you to the museum, on high ground, where an architect's model of the ancient site helps you to visualise the temples. Though shrines have existed on this site since the 17th century BC, Eleusis was renowned in antiquity for its temples and cult of the goddess Demeter, which sprang up circa 1409 BC. The Eleusian Mysteries, by which the faithful were initiated into Demeter's cult, were closely guarded secrets for centuries.

Helpful museum guards will tell you where you may picnic if you've brought your lunch along with you. Alternatively, cafés on the main square in town serve snacks and drinks. Downtown Elefsina café-bars have become trendy in recent years, especially after dark.

To return to Athens, retrace your steps and catch the bus from outside the bakery on the Sacred Way. The trip takes from 40 minutes to an hour, depending on traffic, and the terminus for blue buses from Elefsina (A16, B16) is Koumoundourou/Eleftherias Square.

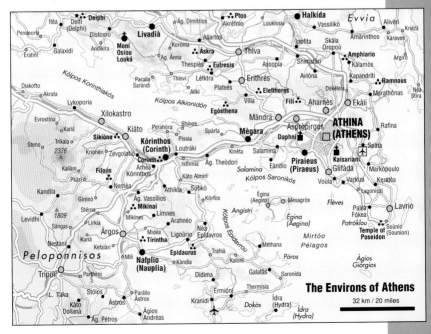

The Environs of Athens

32 km / 20 miles

11: FRIDAY STREET MARKET *(see map below)*

A visit to a fresh vegetable, fruit, fish and flower market in Kolonaki, prefaced by a walk past the Monastery of the Archangels, and followed by a jaunt up to Dexamini Park and lunch at a popular taverna.

This city walking tour begins at the Athens Hilton.

Beginning at around 11am on a Friday from the public fountain (marked by the glass statue of the Olympic runner) in front of the Athens Hilton, cross Vassilissis Sofias Avenue and head uphill on Ioan. Gennadiou Street. Two blocks up from the avenue is the **Monastery of the Archangels/Petraki** (*Moní Petráki*; 5.30am–1.30pm and 5pm–9.30pm, with services daily from 6am–8am, Sun 7am–10am), named after Michael, Gabriel, and the founding family, Petrakis. Stop and take a look at the monastery gardens and lovely frescoes in the 11th–18th-century church. If you are visiting Athens in November, it is worth coming on the 8 November for the monastery's 'Nameday'.

Leave through the monastery gate and turn right up Ioan. Gennadiou Street again. Proceed for a block until the street reaches the **Gennadeion Library** of the **American School of Classical Studies**. This graceful, neo-classical building, with its eight Ionian columns, houses a priceless collection of books on Greece. Turn left on Souidias Street, following signs for Likavitos, and then turn right on Aristodimou Street. Half a block up the hill, you will come to tiny **Dante Square**. Turn left onto Xenokratous, and enter the world of the Athens street market.

For the Senses

The fruit, vegetable and flower market is open in the neighbourhood of Kolonaki from dawn till about 2pm every Friday, rain or shine. Walk through

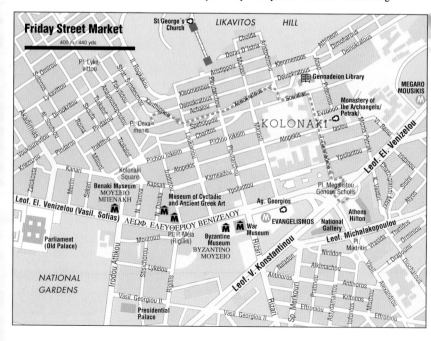

Friday Street Market

the market slowly, keeping your eyes, ears and nose open, while watching out for your shins on the overflowing shopping trolleys. The good quality fresh fruit and vegetables are a lovely sight. Nuts and dried fruits are also a bargain here.

Under an awning on the left, a couple of blocks down Xenokratous, just before you reach the stairs of Ploutarchou Street, stop off at the **spice seller's**. Ask to buy a bag of church incense and a roll of charcoal. If the sweet smell of Greek Orthodox churches appeals to you, it's a scent you can reproduce at home. (See below for instructions on how to do this.)

At No. 19 Xenokratous, on the right down a small flight of steps, you will find **Phillipou's** taverna, a great spot to return to for a very reasonably priced lunch at the end of this walk. The chef is likely to invite you into his kitchen to take a look inside the pots and select your meal. The restaurant is open for lunch from around 1pm onwards.

Proceed along Xenokratous another block. The street changes names here, becoming Xanthippou. Further up Xanthippou, turn left at the Deinokratous Street junction and have coffee in the little pine-scented square of **Dexamenis**, named after the city reservoir constructed here by the Roman Emperor Hadrian. The café here dates from 1900, and has always been a meeting place for the city's lovers, artists and literati. After coffee, the hungry may want to head back to Phillipou's. Shoppers, on the other hand, can proceed down Deinokratous Street to the Kolonaki shopping district. In summer, come back to Dexamenis to go to the open-air cinema here.

Now for the incense: place a disk of charcoal in a heat-proof dish. Hold a lighted match to the disk until it 'catches', and then blow on the charcoal till it glows. Place two or three pellets of incense on the disk, sit back, relax, and enjoy the ecclesiastical scent of jasmine, rose or sandalwood that is released.

Above: monster melons
Right: coffee in Dexamenis Square

12: THE KOUTOUKI CAVE *(see pull-out map)*

A tour of the treasures of Paiania: the Koutouki Cave and the Vorres Museum.

Pack sturdy, non-slip shoes because the cave floor can be hazardous.

Greece's least-known tourist attraction may be its spectacular caves. **The Koutouki Cave** outside the village of **Paiania** is a miniature Carlsbad Cavern on the side of Mount Imitos (Hymettus).

Take the metro, blue line 3, to Ethniki Amina, the last stop. Here, change and take the No. 125 Paiania/Varkiza bus (or take a taxi). Ask your driver

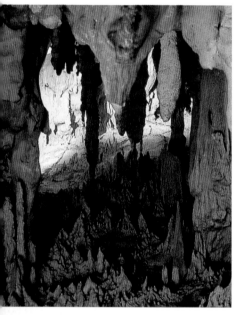

or fellow passengers to let you know when you reach the main square, or *plateía*, in Paiania: the stop is called Agias Triadas. In the square is the Greek Orthodox Church of Zoodohou Pigis, or the 'life-giving spring'. A short walk north of the square is the unique, multifaceted **Vorres Museum** (Sat–Sun 10am–2pm, or by appointment for groups; tel: 210 664-2520; 664-7771; admission charge), which grew out of collector Ion Vorres' private holdings of Greek art. A significant and eclectic collection, spanning Greek art from the Bronze Age to the present, with a special emphasis on contemporary Greek painters, this is a treasure trove of contemporary Greek and folk art.

To the Cave

After seeing the museum (don't miss the folk art collection in the two tower houses forming 'Pyrgi') and taking a stroll in the lovely museum gardens, return to the main square on foot and take a taxi up the side of Mount Imitos to the Koutouki Cave (daily all year 9am–3.45pm; tel: 210 664-2108; 664-2910; admission charge, with reduced fees for children, the elderly and students) about 5km (3 miles) away. Have coffee or ice cream at the little café overlooking the **Mesogeia Plain** while you wait to join one of the half-hourly tours.

The tour of the 3,800 sq m (40,000 sq ft) cave takes approximately 20 minutes – watch your step, as it's slippery. The interior, rich with polychromatic stalactites and stalagmites, is dramatically lit to create beautiful special effects

The intrepid may want to walk down. It's an hour on foot back to Paiania and the bus stop, and be warned, it is very hot in full summer. Those who enjoy the Koutouki may want to buy Ann Petrocheilou's *The Greek Caves*, available at the café/gift shop outside the cave entrance.

Above: the Koutouki Cave
Right: the Temple of Olympian Zeus

13: CIRCLING THE GARDENS *(see pull-out map)*

Morning at the Temple of Olympian Zeus, followed by a stroll through the Zappeion and a visit to the Panathenaic Stadium and lunch in the National Gardens.

Begin at Vasilissis Amalias Avenue at the level of Dionysiou Areopagitou Street. The nearest metro stations are Akropoli and Syntagma.

Start at the **Arch of Hadrian** on Vasilissis Amalias Avenue. On the Acropolis side of the arch, an inscription reads: 'Here is Athens, the ancient city of Theseus'. On the other side, the Emperor Hadrian had inscribed in AD 132: 'This is the city of Hadrian; not of Theseus'.

Walk through the arch and turn left up a dirt path which quickly turns into tarmac. On your left, as you enter Vasilissis Olgas Avenue, is a statue of **Byron**, that great philhellene, in the arms of Greece. Half a block down, turn right into the Archaeological Site of Olympeion (or **The Temple of Olympian Zeus**; daily 8am–3pm, closed Mon; tel: 210 922-6330; admission charge). The massive temple, the largest in mainland Greece, honouring the father of the gods was under construction for some 650 years, and was finally completed by Hadrian in AD 132. The 15 extant columns, 27m (90ft) high, give the visitor some idea of the enormous dimensions of the original structure.

If you want a more precise idea of what Athens' ruined temples looked like in the Golden Age, pick up a copy of *Athens Past and Present*, by Niki Drossou Panaiotou, available at the Eleftheroudakis book shop at 4 Nikis Street. In this ingenious book, the reconstructions of the ancient monuments are depicted on film overlaying photographs of the ruins.

Garden Stroll

Leave the site through the entrance gate and cross Vasilissis Olgas at the pedestrian crosswalk. Walk up the broad, tree-lined approach to the park and bear right in front of the impressive, neoclassical building where the Council of Europe meets, the **Zappeion**, named after the two brothers who

donated the edifice. Pass between the Zappeion and the Aigli Bistro café, and turn right at the next junction of paths. Proceed under a canopy of laurel and flowering Judas trees, past a statue of a cherub with a violin, until you reach the equestrian statue of Revolutionary War General Karaiskakis. The inscription on the statue reads: 'I am dying: You remain united and support the homeland'. Ahead of you is a small bronze statue of a discus thrower; beyond is the newly refurbished **Panathenaic Stadium**, or Pan-Athenian Stadium. Built in 1870, to a design by Ernst Ziller, this was the site of the first modern Olympiad in 1896. The stadium is a good place to jog, though the smog here is heavy as early as 5.30am. The Stadium, popularly known as the Kalimármaro, was one of the somewhat self-aggrandising gifts Marathon millionaire Herod Atticus made to his adopted city between AD 139 and 144. Laid out in the form of a Roman stadium, this arena is semi-circular; it seated some 50,000 spectators of such events as the capital city's Panathenaic Festivals – spectacles featuring wild animals.

The Presidential Palace

Returning back towards the gardens from the stadium, head down Irodou Attikou Street. On your right, *évzone* guards are posted in sentry boxes outside the **Palace**, formerly Royal, now Presidential, which was also designed by Ernst Ziller in the 1890s. On your left, two-thirds of the way up Irodou Attikou, where Lykeiou Street intersects, you can enter the gardens through a green iron gate. A little **café** *(kafeneíon)* straddles the path. Stop here for a snack. This is a lovely place to rest and is frequented mainly by locals. The **Botanical Museum** (Tues–Sun 9am–3pm, closed Mon) is a stone's throw away from here, and showcases the National Gardens' rarest holdings.

After dipping into the museum, wander in the gardens, laid out by Queen Amalia in the 1840s, with their 7,000m (7,600yds) of walkways, offering the perfect antidote for smog inhalation and travel-frazzled nerves. There are exits in all four directions, and signs directing visitors back to Syntagma Square.

Above: the National Gardens
Right: the Zappeion

14: AN ORTHODOX MORNING *(see pull-out map)*

A visit to three Greek Orthodox churches in central Athens, the Philokalia book shop and the Chapel of St George atop Mount Likavitos.

Dress appropriately for entering the churches. This means skirts and sleeves for women.

Begin this tour at the Syntagma Square Post Office before 11am. Walk down Mitropoleos Street. Cross Nikis, Voulis, Pentelis, Patrooü and Ypatias streets (all in the course of approximately two city blocks), and you will find yourself in the **Cathedral Square**. The structure dominating the square is the **Church of the Annunciation**, Athens' cathedral. Completed in 1862, it took 20 years to build and was designed, as it were, by committee.

Directly next door, nestled up against the massive cathedral, is a much more human-scaled bastion against sin, the 12th-century **Gorgoepikoös**, or **Agios Eleftherios**. The anonymous architect of this beautiful structure may well have attended services atop the Acropolis when the Parthenon was the city's Christian meeting place. The Gorgoepikoös (the name means 'Virgin Swift to Hear') may have been sacred to women in childbirth or perhaps the private chapel of the Archbishop. The construction materials for the church included fragments of pagan temples once located nearby, as well as reliefs from earlier 6th- and 7th-century Christian churches.

Heading back up Mitropoleos Street towards Syntagma Square, call in at minuscule **Agia Dynami**, the chapel sheltering under the Ministry of Education building at the corner of Mitropoleos and Pentelis Streets. At the next corner, turn right onto Voulis Street. At No. 36 is the **Philokalia book shop** (9am–3.30pm, Tues till 6.30pm), where visitors can find books on the Greek faith (Timothy Ware's *The Greek Orthodox Church* is a particularly revealing source of information), quality icons, Christmas and Easter cards, incense burners, cassettes of church music, etc.

Mount Likavitos

Retracing your steps to Mitropoleos Street, turn right and head uphill to Syntagma Square. Hail a taxi and ask for the Likavitos *teleferique*. This is the tiny **funicular railway** which scales the small peak of Mount Likavitos.

Buy a (reasonable) round-trip ticket (or go one way and walk down). The train (daily 9am–11.45pm) will take you up to the top of Likavitos, crowned by the whitewashed Chapel of St George ('Nameday', 23 April). Linger for snacks or a meal on the summit. After dark, this is a lovely vantage point from which to savour Athens' million points of light.

Right: Greek Orthodoxy is alive and well

15: THE NATIONAL
ARCHAEOLOGICAL MUSEUM *(see pull-out map)*

A guided, or independent, tour of the 'Athenian Louvre'.

Take the metro to Victoria and walk down Patision Street. As the museum has been closed for renovations, check opening times before setting out.

The **National Archaeological Museum** (44 Patision Street, tel: 210 821-7724, www.culture.gr; summer Mon 12.30pm–7pm, Tues–Fri 8am–7pm, Sat–Sun 8.30am–3pm; winter Mon 11–5pm, Tues–Fri 8am–5pm, Sat–Sun 8.30am–3pm) is a vast structure, built between 1850 and 1889. It houses an incredible wealth of ancient Greek art, dating from the Neolithic-Age Collection through to Hellenistic and Graeco-Roman artefacts. At this writing, and for well over a year leading up to the 2004 Olympics, the museum has been closed while being extensively renovated. When the museum again opens to the public, it is expected that the rather lacklustre presentation of decades past will have been replaced by something more dynamic.

For help taking it all in, turn to Basil Petrakos' book, *National Museum: Sculpture – Bronzes – Vases*, which provides good room-by-room descriptions. The professional guides, sitting to your right as you enter, provide tours in English, French, German, Spanish or Italian.

Of special interest are the **Cycladic Collection** of Bronze-Age marbles and the **Mycenaean Collection** of gold artefacts which includes gold death masks such as the incorrectly labelled **'Mask of Agamemnon'**, found at Mycenae and dating from the 16th century BC, long before the Trojan Wars. Also of particular interest is the bronze **Poseidon**; the life-size bronze horse in flight from the 2nd century BC; the bronze **Youth of Antikythera**, *circa* 340 BC, with his inlaid eyes and lovingly rendered lashes.

The **Egyptian Rooms** are beautifully displayed. Also well worth a look, and equally well laid out, is the **Stathatos Collection** of gold in the adjoining gallery. Donated in 1971 by Helen Stathatos, this contains items from a large span of Greek history, from Cycladic and Mycenean pieces, to Roman and Byzantine works.

Fine Souvenirs

The basement museum shop is one of the best places for finely crafted souvenirs in Greece, and includes replicas from other museums in the country. Next door is the museum's café which overlooks a sculpture garden – a good place to cool your aching heels after trudging round the museum.

Above: the 'Mask of Agamemnon'. **Left:** 7th century BC statue
Right: cinema in the open air

16: AN OPEN-AIR CINEMA WITH A VIEW AND DINNER IN PLAKA *(see map, p50)*

See a vintage film in Plaka, the old city, and enjoy guitar music with your dinner at Xynou, an old Plaka taverna.

For other open-air cinemas in the city, consult the weekly newspaper The Athens News.

In the 1950s and 1960s, before the widespread availability of television and air-conditioning, attending an open-air cinema, with the film starting just after dusk on a hot summer's evening, was a treat for wage-earning Athenians stuck in the sweltering city while their more fortunate wives and children had retreated to the islands. Apartment dwellers in the immediate vicinity would move out on to their balconies to catch the show. Then, after the movie (epics such as *El Cid* and *Ben Hur* particularly spring to mind), as the evening cooled, Athenians would repair to a local, open-air taverna, staying until the wee hours with their *paréa*, a small group of lifelong friends.

Getting There

At about 8pm, start at Syntagma's main Post Office, and follow Filellinon Street away from the square for approximately three blocks. Turn right down Kydathinaion Street, the pedestrian walkway into Plaka. Pass the Church of the Saviour on your right, cross Monis Asteriou/Sotiros Street, and then cross little Aggelou Geronta Street, which will bring you to Plaka's central square, Plateia Filomousou Etaireias, filled on warm evenings with tables of diners enjoying *retsína, mezédes* and the passing parade.

At No. 22 Kydathinaion is the **Ciné Paris** open-air cinema, an Athens landmark which shows vintage films in their original versions all summer from around the second week of May to the end of the first week in October. Screenings are usually at 8.45pm and 11pm; while you wait you can sip a beer

and enjoy an excellent view of the Acropolis from the rooftop bar.

After the film, exit onto Kydathinaion again, and turn left. Retrace your steps and turn left onto Aggelou Geronta Street. At the end of a short block, before you reach Ag. Hatzimihali Street, you'll see an alley leading to a green lattice fence. Here is the taverna **Xynou**, open since 1936, and not much changed. Xynou is closed at weekends and in July, but at other times it's a treat between 8pm and 1am, with good wine from the barrel and guitar music.

If you find Xynou closed, return to the main square and eat at the one good, honest taverna there, **Byzantino**, No. 18 Kydathinaion, a great place to people-watch before wandering down Adrianou Street to experience after-hours Plaka. Another dining option in Plaka is **Platanos** (4 Diogenous Street, near the Tower of the Winds, tel: 210 322-0666). Alternatively, walk up the Marasli Street steps of Mount Likavitos till you come to Aristippou Street: at No. 44 is an excellent taverna, **Rodia** (closed Sun, tel: 210 722-9883). Its veal in lemon sauce, *lemonáto*, lamb in oregano sauce, *rigonáto*, and the cheese croquettes are all recommended, as is the barrel wine. You may be treated to acoustic guitar music in the garden.

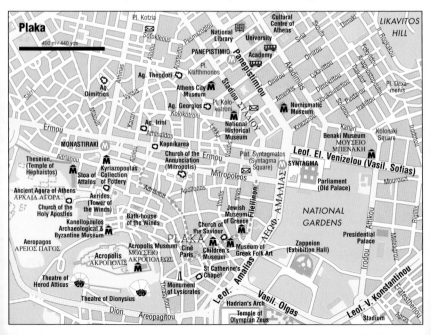

17: PAMPERING AND PILATES *(see pull-out map)*

As an antidote to museum-hopping and ruin-wading, sample beauty treatments and alternative therapies in the Kolonaki district.

Kolonaki, the central residential and shopping district of Athens, radiating out from Kolonaki Square *(Plateía Filikís Etairías)* and presided over by the mini-massif Mount Likavitos, is Athens' equivalent to London's Sloane Street or Los Angeles' Rodeo Drive. Kolonaki Square was named after a Roman column *(kolóna)* once located in the area and also after a secret brotherhood (*Filikís Etairías* means 'Friendly Association') of Greek patriots, established in 1814, whose mission was to free Greece from the yoke of the Ottoman Turk. Many of the same internationally famous patriots' names are still to be found on the street signs of Kolonaki.

At 12 Iraklitou Street (first floor) is Vanessa Iliopoulou's lively and friendly salon/spa called **Giel Haute Coiffure** (Tues, Thur, Fri 8.30am–6pm, Wed 8.30am–3pm, Sat 8am–4.30pm, closed Mon; tel: 210 360-8089/210 360-2955 for appointments), where female visitors may retreat for hair colouring and styling, sugar waxing, pedicures, manicures and make-overs. Prices are extraordinarily reasonable, but no plastic is accepted: cash only, and do remember to tip individuals 10–20 percent for good service.

At 18 Dimoharous Street is Jenny Colebourne's **Illium Centre of Light** (tel: 210 723-1397, email: illium@hol.gr for an appointment). In this lovely townhouse retreat, customers can sign up for a Pilates session, or sit in on a Hatha yoga class. Among the other options often on offer are shiatsu, aromatherapy, chiropody, Reiki, reflexology and many other alternative therapies: just the thing to revive weary travellers.

Jenny Colebourne, a British-born dancer who has lived in Athens for more than two decades, introduced Pilates-style body control to Greece. This low-impact strengthening technique (demonstrated right) is based on precise stretching/movement and was originally developed in New York by Joseph Pilates to accelerate the recovery and reconditioning of injured athletes and dancers. The exercise has gained worldwide recognition in the past decade. The Illium Centre of Light makes a convivial place to experience Pilates on a one-to-one basis.

Colebourne is a certified Reiki Master (qualified to lead Reiki retreats and to train and initiate other Reiki practitioners), as well as a skilled Cranio-Sacral therapist. Her clients include many prominent Athenians who support alternative modes of healing.

Left: dining in Plaka
Above: performing Pilates

THE OLYMPICS COME HOME

Athens, accustomed graciously to welcoming foreign visitors for some three millennia will, between 13 and 29 August 2004, open wide its arms to some 5.3 million ticketed spectators, 10,500 athletes, and tens of thousands of media representatives, team officials, volunteers and diaspora Greeks who have come to attend, or compete in, the Summer Games of the 2004 Olympics.

To prepare for the Olympiad, Athens, which hadn't hosted the Games since it staged the inaugural Games of 1896, pulled out all the stops. Seem-

ingly overnight, if several years late (the bid was won in 1997), the capital shifted into fifth gear and mounted a sustained campaign of demolition, building, restoring, re-routing and beautifying. Occasionally, gears bounced into reverse – Omonia Square was torn up and re-designed but, when no one liked the results, torn up, reimagined and re-built yet again – but the direction was ever forward, ever upward, with no time to lose.

There are at least two major city centre works of which all seem to approve: the expanded currently 19-station, three-line metro system, which has made commuting in three directions, Sepolia to Dáfni to Ethniki Amynta, such a pleasure; and the so-called 'Unification of the Archaeological Sites of Athens,' project, a Golden-Age-of-Athens-pedestrianised-promenade which enables strollers to amble around the ancient sites while taking in a bare minimum of vehicle exhaust. Also, everyone, save the city's taxi drivers, likes the new

The Ancient Games

Only one among many 'pan-Hellenic festivals' celebrated in antiquity, the Olympic Games probably date from only 720 BC, though the 'official' date is usually given as 776 BC. Every four years for over a thousand years, the Peloponnesian city-state of Olympia hosted a festive competition to honour the father of the gods, Zeus of Mt Olympus. In the beginning, there was but one athletic event, a race to the altar of Zeus. And, from the beginning as well, there was the Sacred Truce (Ekecheiria), marked by a cessation of hostilities amongst participants for the duration of the Games, a ceasefire which dates from the 8th century BC, when the rulers of Elis, Pisa and Sparta agreed to its terms. Still, for the ancients, the "Olympics turned out to be war continued through other means," in the words of Michael Macrone (author of *It's Greek To Me*). Winning was all, and the victors could eat out on their awards for life. (When you think of such Olympic medalists as Nadia Comaneci and Jean-Claude Killy, not much has changed.)

Top: the start of the 100 metres race at the inaugural Olympiad, held in Athens in 1896

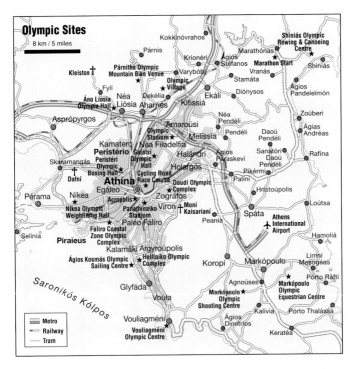

athens & environs

airport in Spata; and the new tramline to the coast, which will whisk bathers from the steamy Zappeion to Glifada in record time, will be another boon to the city. There are also state-of-the-art athletic venues dotting the city and the province of Attica.

Tickets and Accommodation

Upon the launch of sales, 5.3 million tickets were made available; 3 million to the general public in the EU and EEA; 2.3 million to national Olympic committees, and other contractual client groups. Tickets can be had through the official ticketing website (www.athens2004.com/tickets) or by calling, tel: 210 373-0000. They range in cost from €10–60.

Athens has gone to extraordinary lengths to provide accommodation for the huge projected influx of visitors. Eleven cruise ships, including the *Queen Mary II*, will comprise a deluxe floating dormitory off Piraeus, the *Queen Mary* alone accommodating 13,000 visitors. Filoxenia '04 will manage a private homes rental programme, providing reasonably priced lodging in a wide range of residences (www.filoxenia.com). And though the majority of Athens hotel rooms have now been booked long in advance of the Games, local travel agents can still find space in Attica for attendees, though visitors and officials will be commuting from as far away as Evia and Andros.

Those interested in an in-depth and authoritative account of the Olympics, in all their glory and complexity, should read David Miller's *Athens to Athens: The Official History of the Olympic Games and the IOC, 1894–2004*. The official website of the 2004 Olympics is www.athens2004.gr.

Excursions

EXCURSION 1: A DAY ON HYDRA *(see pull-out map)*

Take the Flying Dolphin to the island of Hydra.

Be warned: visitors tend to dress up rather than down for the beach and café life here. Maps of the island, available in Hydra Town, will enable you to navigate the warren of vertical streets that make up the port and make your way to coastal coves and swimming spots.

Flying Dolphins (hydrofoils) and catamarans leave for the Saronic Gulf island of **Hydra** (pronounced Ee-thra) from Piraeus from 8am daily. It is advisable to buy a return ticket, as the craft are packed to the brim in high season. The round trip fare will be about €35, and the journey will take about 2 hours, making a stop at Poros. Since the schedules vary seasonally, and according to weather conditions, call Hellas Flying Dolphins (tel: 210 419-9200) for up-to-the-minute information. Take along a bathing suit, sunblock, towel and a hat in summer, and allow at least an hour to reach Piraeus from central Athens.

Hydreia (the 'water-rich' isle) was settled in the 15th century by mainland, Peloponnesian Greeks fleeing the Ottoman Turks, followed by successive waves of Albanians in the 18th century. Long a maritime centre known for its prosperous sea-captains – and not a few pirates – Hydra played a major role in the Greek War of Independence, supplying 190 of the nascent country's 290 warships when hostilities broke out on 25 March, 1821.

Timeless Hydra

Today, the island still seems caught in the amber of the 18th to 19th centuries owing to protective building laws and the dearth of wheeled traffic. The little horseshoe-shaped harbour town, also called Hydra, is the island's hub, with its sea captains' mansions standing alongside elegant boutiques and cafés. In the centre of the harbour, don't miss the 18th-century **Monastery of the Panagia Mitropoleos** with its marble belltower and cloister. And ask the way to the swimming grotto at the end of the port (there are other swimming coves further along the 'corniche') if you fancy a dip.

For hikers, the hilltop monasteries of the Prophet Ilias, St Efpraxia and the Holy Trinity are more than an hour's rigorous climb, but worth it for the view, especially at sundown.

Good places to eat are Mezodopoleion To Paradosiakon, a family-run taverna up from the port, and Taverna Tis Kondilenias, a 10 minute walk along the paved coastal path towards **Vlychos** (water taxis make this journey in a minute, and can whisk you off to other hamlets and beaches round the island).

Left: the horseshoe-shaped harbour at Hydra
Right: transport Hydra-style

EXCURSION 2: ANCIENT CORINTH *(see pull-out map)*

A full day or overnight train or bus trip to Ancient Corinth, the ancient site, the medieval fortress, and dinner at a local taverna.

Take the train for leisurely enjoyment or the bus if you're pressed for time.

Ancient Corinth (Ancient Corinth Archaeological Site and Corinth Museum; summer 8am–7pm; winter, 8am–5pm; admission charge) is about 85km (53 miles) from Athens, and represents a

pleasant day trip. The village proper is accessible by bus from the modern city of Corinth, 8 km (5 miles) from Ancient Corinth. Buses leave Corinth every hour on the hour from 6.15am till 9pm, and return every hour on the half hour till 9.30pm. Alternatively, take the metro to Stathmos Larisis for the Peloponnisos Train Station, or take a taxi or bus to the intercity bus station on the Kifissos River. The train journey from Athens to modern Corinth takes around three hours; the bus journey takes 1½ hours, sometimes less. If enjoying the journey is as important to you as getting there, take the train. If not, take the faster, more efficient bus. Either way, don't miss seeing the **Corinth Canal**: ask a fellow passenger to alert you in good time. The canal, cutting through the isthmus linking the Peloponnese to the mainland is a spectacular sight, which comes and goes in the space of three seconds.

Known in antiquity for its wealth and its debauchery, Corinth was a sea-power in the 8th to 6th centuries BC and survived successive switches of allegiance between Sparta and Athens, depending on which way the winds of power were blowing. Destroyed by Rome in 146 BC, it was rebuilt, in 46 BC, by Julius Caesar. Then came St Paul, to save what Caesar had not. But what

conquerors of all sorts could not lay waste or pillage, earthquakes finally brought down. A particularly violent quake convinced inhabitants of Corinth to relocate their city from the ancient site to the isthmus. Today, Ancient Corinth – primarily Roman-era remains – is some 5km (3 miles) west of Modern Corinth.

In Corinth, the bus for Ancient Corinth leaves from the bus station where your Athens connection drops you. Train passengers will have a 10-minute walk from the railway station to the bus station: ask a porter in Corinth railway station to direct you, or take a taxi.

The Site

The bus connection from modern to Ancient Corinth takes about 15 minutes. Get off in the village square *(Ee plateía tis Archéas Kórinthou)*. Here have coffee and/or breakfast at the **Yemelos Restaurant** (tel: 27410 31361) before heading up to the site of the extensive Greek and Roman antiquities (daily 8am–7pm). Note the impressive Archaic Hellenic temple in severe Doric style, dedicated to the god Apollo, and the idyllic setting of the Roman Odeon or theatre. There is also a small but good museum located within the ar-

chaeological area. The entrance to the site is less than five minutes' walk from the Yemelos and the admission charge covers both site and museum.

In addition to the ancient site, there is the medieval **fortress of Acrocorinth**, located atop the lofty, lone mountain. A paved road winds up to the entrance to the castle, where ruins date from the 6th century BC through to the 19th century. Catch a taxi in the village square or, if you are feeling energetic, walk up to the Acropolis. Allow at least two hours to explore Acrocorinth. Wear sturdy shoes and be prepared for some tricky footwork. Do not, under any circumstances, stay in the castle after dark: the terrain is extremely hazardous, with dangerous pitfalls and deep cisterns.

A restaurant at the castle entrance sells drinks and meals. The round-trip taxi fare is quite expensive, so you might consider walking down if you have the time and energy. It's a beautiful route, especially at dusk. For those staying on through dinner, there are two other worthwhile places to eat in addition to the Yemelos (which also rents out rooms): first, the restaurant **Dionysos** (open 10.30am–1pm for breakfast; then, from 7pm–12.30am for dinner; tel: 27410 31579), northeast of the square, just past the church (ask locals); and second, a taverna opposite Dionysos called **Tassos** (open all day; tel: 27410 31225).

For current information concerning train schedules, call in at 6 Sina Street, tel: 210 529-7313.

Top Left: take the train. **Left:** the Corinth Canal
Right: ancient Corinth

EXCURSION 3: DELPHI *(see pull-out map)*

Take the bus to the ancient Sanctuary of Apollo at Delphi.

This beautiful site is best seen over a two-day period.

It is possible to see Delphi in one day, but the site is best seen at a more leisurely pace, and there are many good hotels close by. Buses for Delphi leave at regular intervals, six daily, from the Liosion Street bus station (north of Larissa railway station; best reached by taxi; call KTEL for information on 210 831-7096) and the journey takes around 3 hours. It is best to book your return ticket as soon as possible, to avoid a long wait.

Delphi (Mon 8.30am–2.45pm, Tues–Sun 7.30am–6.45pm; tel: 22650 82312; admission charge), the site of both the **Oracle** and the **Temple of Apollo**, dates from the 4th century BC, but has been a holy site since the 14th–11th centuries BC, when Gaia (Earth) was worshipped here. It is an exquisite spot, especially in winter and spring, when the mountainside temple site is less overrun with tourists. Located on terraced hills beneath twin-peaked Mount Parnassos, Delphi was considered the *omphalos* ('world's navel'), the meeting point of two eagles despatched by Zeus to find the centre of the earth. The mountain village of **Arachova** – in winter, a haven for skiers – which may be visited on the way to or from Athens, is very pretty. It is away from the main road (a hike uphill), and you can enjoy browsing in shops selling woollens, local crafts and Greek honey.

The site consists of the Sacred Precinct, the seat of Delphi's famous oracle, and the Sanctuary of Athena (where the circular **Tholos** – Delphi's most photographed building – can be found). You enter the Sacred Precinct along the Sacred Way, the road by which the

Above: Temple of Apollo, Delphi
Right: the bronze charioteer still retains his onyx eyes

pilgrims approached the main temple. The way was lined with niches containing thousands of statues (offerings from various Greek city states). One of the most impressive is the Treasury of the Athenians (on the left as you turn the corner going up the hill), built to celebrate the Athenian victory over the Persians at Marathon in 490BC.

The oracle herself – a local woman who delivered the prophecies – resided in the large Temple of Apollo, which lies at the end of the Sacred Way. Within the Doric order temple was the cleft over which the priestess was suspended as she prophesied (the cleft was probably volcanic and the fumes may have induced the oracle's trance-like state). By the Sacred Precinct, is the fine **Delphi Museum** (daily 8.30am–2.45pm; free admission), now beautifully renovated, which houses the famous bronze charioteer.

Leaving the Sacred Precinct and walking along the road towards Arachova you come – on the left – to the **Castalian Spring**, where pilgrims would purify themsleves before carrying on to the the temple. Further on, and this time on the right, is the **Sanctuary of Athena** (summer 7.30am–8pm; winter 7.30am–sunset; free admission). The temple to the goddess can only be traced by its foundations, but the Tholos has been partially reconstructed.

EXCURSION 4: SELF-DRIVE VISIT TO GALAXIDI (VIA DELPHI) *(see pull-out map)*

At least an overnight visit to the 19th-century port town of Galaxidi, via the mountain site of Delphi and village of Arachova.

Take swimsuits, non-slip shoes, sea shoes (there are sea urchins at Galaxidi) and sun hats for Delphi, where there is little shade.

This overnight excursion to **Galaxidi**, a charming port town on the **Gulf of Corinth**, a 230-km (145-mile) trip northwest of Athens, may be combined with a morning/early afternoon exploration of Delphi *(see facing page)*, plus a visit to the Delphi Museum. Buses to Galixidi operate from either Delphi, Amfissa or Itea; the latter two are a short bus journey or taxi ride from Delphi.

Call and reserve rooms at either the newly renovated **Ganimede Hotel** (33052 Galaxidion, tel: 22650 41328, fax: 22650 42160; €€), or the attractive **Hotel Argo** (33052 Galaxidion, tel: 22650 41996/42100, fax: 22650 41878; €€), a pleasant, beautifully renovated, C-class hotel of 30 rooms, some housed in a 19th-century villa complete with modern comforts such as air-conditioning and TV. However, the Ganimede, also air-conditioned, has more personality. Both hotels are reasonably priced, although the breakfast-in-the-garden at the Ganimede is a bonus.

Right: an easy charm

Through Mount Parnassos

About an hour north of Athens, the bus turns off for Thiva/Livadia/Delphi and passes through the villages of Aliartos and Agia Paraskevi. The signs point towards Delphi/Arachova, the latter being the skiing village on the slopes of Mount Parnassos (Parnassus), sacred to the Muses, companions to the god Apollo, which you will reach before Delphi. You pass through two tunnels through the rock, the massif of Mount Parnassos rising before you, the road lined with pink and white oleander and the spears of cypress trees.

Some 150–160km (90–95 miles) out of Athens, you will reach **Arachova**, which is well worth a visit. In the last shady square on the main road, try

the *peinerli* (pay-nair-lee), a sort of croissant stuffed with cheese and bacon, at the **Café Bon Jour** (tel: 22650 31926). For lunch, wait till Delphi, and the **Epikouros Restaurant** (tel: 22650 83250).

Four kilometres (2½ miles) further on, you will reach Delphi. One fee covers both museum and temple site (see *Delphi Excursion, page 58*), so hold on to your tickets. Do not miss a tiny side room in the museum which houses remarkable, 6th-century BC ivory and gold heads of (perhaps) Apollo and his sister, Artemis. One kilometre (½ mile) after the archaeological site, there is a spectacular view of the plain below from the modern town of Delphi.

On to Galixidi

From Delphi, the descent begins to the Gulf of Corinth, traversing an immense and ancient grove of olives on the way to Itea. Ten kilometres (6 miles) out of Delphi is the turning for Itea/Galaxidi. Twenty kilometres (12 miles) further on is **Galaxidi**.

After checking in to your hotel *(see page 59 for recommendations)*, explore the town. A maritime hub of great renown in the 18th and 19th centuries, it is impressive today for its lovely 19th-century architecture, its twin ports, pebbly beaches, good tavernas, pensions, cafés and shops. On the waterfront of the main harbour you will find a little *ouzeri*/taverna called **The Beautiful Greece** *(Ee Oréa Ellás)*, 79 Akti Oianthis, 33052 Paraleia Galaxidion, tel. 22650 42016). Among the many mouthwatering dishes on the menu, try their beets and garlic sauce, fried whitebait, grilled octopus and greens.

Two special gift shops on the waterfront are also highly recommended: **Mr Kosmas P Dimitriadis's** jewellery shop and, a few doors down, **Ostria**, a gift and antiques shop with model ships, hand-painted ceramics, jewellery and toys.

Above: splash out in Galaxidi
Right: the Sanctuary of Athena at Delphi

Leisure Activities

SHOPPING

Arts & Antiques

Although it is illegal to remove any object (even seemingly insignificant potsherds) from ancient sites in Athens, or anywhere else in Greece for that matter, buyers may still obtain permits to export certain antiquities. Byzantine icons, antique jewellery, costumes, embroidered fabrics, folk crafts, china and pottery, coins, stamps, etchings, books – all are available, for a price, but are best purchased from experienced antiquarians who can help with obtaining permits and authentication.

All but collectors, however, will probably be satisfied with excellent modern copies of such things as Skyrian chests and chairs, carved shepherds' crooks, silver-chased icons and Cycladic seed-pearl and gold earrings. These latter-day versions require no complicated dealings with the authorities to be able to transport them out of the country – and no alarm system at home. They are also easy on the wallet.

But if it's the real thing you're after, **Monastiraki's Flea Market** is known for its knowledgeable denizens. **Eleni Martinou**, at 50 Pandrossou Street (tel: 210 321-2414), is the accepted Monastiraki authority on all things that are both antique and Greek. Ms. Martinou has another shop, located in the upscale Kolonaki shopping district, at 24 Pindarou Street (tel: 210 360-9449; 360-7230).

Peggy Zoumboulakis is another Kolonaki antiquarian and gallerist. **Gallery Zoumboulakis**, at 26 Haritos Street in Kolonaki (tel: 210 725-2488) offers antique furniture, household objects, jewellery, embroideries and silver. Another Zoumboulakis gallery, at 7 Kriezotou Street (tel: 210 363-4454), is a fruitful place to visit as well, but for contemporary Greek art as opposed to antiques. This shop, and the main Zoumboulakis gallery on Kolonaki Square (tel:

210 360-8278) are best known for exhibiting and selling contemporary paintings in oil and acrylics, prints, posters and small sculptures.

Contemporary art is often an excellent buy in Athens, and there are many good galleries showing the work of Greek artists such as Mytaras, Moralis, Fassianos, Psychopedis, Tsarouchis and others worth seeing. You may also want to check such publications as *The Athens News* and the *Kathimerini* insert in *The International Herald Tribune* for the dates and times of upcoming shows and gallery openings in Athens. You will be made to feel very welcome at any of these festive and fashionable events.

Crafts, Museum Copies and Olympics Souvenirs

Folk arts and crafts are the most desirable purchases in Athens, whether you're interested in fluffy white *flokáti* rugs, hand-knotted carpets in traditional patterns, silver filigree jewellery from Ioannina, or carved wooden furniture. **The National Welfare Organisation**, at 6 Ipatias Street in the centre (tel: 210 324-0017), offers the full gamut of Greek crafts, especially carpets, under one roof.

The Centre of Hellenic Tradition, at 56 Mitropoleos and 36 Pandrossou streets (tel: 210 321-3023), offers a potpourri of traditional Hellenic crafts, with a sprinkling of antiques, furniture and marble architectural elements. Worth seeking out in the basement of the **National Archaeological Museum**, at 44 Patission Street, is a fine shop stocking museum copies, particularly statuary (tel: 210 821-7717; 210 821-7724). The **Benaki Museum** and the **Museum of Cycladic and Ancient**

Left: flea market on Ermou
Right: replica vase

Greek Art both have excellent shops which are good places to purchase gifts.

In Plaka, at 142 Adrianou Street, Yorgos Roumantzis' **Archipelagos** (tel: 210 323-1321) has delectable small gifts, ceramics and jewellery, which are very reasonably priced.

Tanagrea (26 Voulis and 15 Mitropoleos streets, tel: 210 322-3366) features sophisticated versions of traditional Greek charms against the Evil Eye, handpainted ceramics, and fine pewter items. **Olive Wood** (8 Mnisikleous Street, tel: 210 321-6145) sells sculptor/playwright Vangelis Rikoudis' olive and drift wood creations: clever ships, bowls, candelabra, fish worrybeads and kitchen utensils. A must! Finally, for Olympic and absolutely all other souvenirs, head for **Shopping Center Plaka** (1 Pandrossou Street, tel: 210 324-5405, email: shoppap@otenet.gr).

Greek Gold

Athens is justly renowned for its jewellery rendered in 22-carat gold. The big-name goldsmiths and some smaller names all have stunning collections. Lesser known jewellers such as Fanourakis or Minas may charge more than Lalaounis and Zolotas (see *below*), but you won't see their creations on others in New York and Paris.

Greece's self-styled 'ambassador of gold' is **Ilias Lalaounis**, with stores at 6 Panepistimiou Street (tel: 210 362-4354), the Athens Tower, Eleftherios Venizelos International Airport, and elsewhere in the city. Be sure to see Lalaounis' household objects and silver services as well, as these are unusual and not widely known outside of Greece.

To get a better idea of the extent of Ilias Lalaounis' artistry, visit the **Ilias Lalaounis Jewellery Museum**, 12 Kallisperi and Karyatidon streets, near the Acropolis (Mon, Thur, Fri and Sat 9am–4pm, Wed 9am–9pm, Sun 10am–2pm, closed Tues; tel: 210 922-1044). The permanent collection comprises some 3,000 designs; the **museum shop** can satisfy all your desires for

Greek gold – and then some. Of particular interest is a video presentation which explains various types of fine work with gold: chain braiding, filigree and granulation.

Some of the most unusual gold work in Athens is done by the designers at **Fanourakis**, which has shops at 23 Patriarchou Ioacheim Street in Kolonaki (tel: 210 721-1762), 2 Evangelistrias Street in the city centre, and 6 Panagitsas Street in Kifissia. Unusually cut and pavé diamonds, gold-treated-as-fabric, and whimsical bows and insects are this jeweller's signatures. Fanourakis' work is also feminine and light enough to wear, which cannot be said of the majority of the gold-by-the-kilo work in Athens. The Fanourakis family, with roots in Iraklio, Crete, boasts 130 years of uninterrupted artistry in gold. The latest artist in residence is **Lina Fanouraki,** whose understanding of women makes her line so appealing.

If your tastes run to the extremely stylised botanical forms available at Tiffany & Co. in the US, you should see the work in gold and silver by **Minas**. On your excursion to Hydra (see *page 55*), visit the shop of **Likourgos Keramidas, Greco Gold**, at the port (tel: 02980 53012) and ask to see a selection of Minas' distinctive large cufflinks, rings, ankle bracelets, etc. (Minas also maintains a shop on Mykonos.)

Chic Boutiques in Kolonaki

The nexus of streets around **Kolonaki Square**, or the Plateia Filikis Etairias, forms the most interesting, concentrated, up-market shopping district in central Athens: this is definitely not the area for tourist T-shirts and plastic worrybeads. Here are the posh foreign boutiques (Armani, Cartier, DKNY, Max Mara), plus homegrown ones such as **Aslanis** (clothing; 16 Anagnostopoulou and Irakleitou streets), **Free Shop** (clothing; 75 Haritos Street), **Folli Follie** (jewellery; 25 Solonos Street) and myriad other small Greek emporia for fine clothing, accessories and furnishings.

One of my favourite Greek gift shops is called **Etc.,** located in Kolonaki just off Patriarchou Ioacheim Street at 21 Loukianou Street (tel: 210 723-4720). Here you will find Greek votive offerings

Left: lace-making. **Top Right:** just browsing.
Right: modern iconography

(*támata*) in silver, silver wedding 'crowns' for the Greek marriage ceremony (*stéffana*) and candles, beads, whimsical costume jewellery and baby charms against the Evil Eye: all very Greek, but styled for modern, urban tastes.

Allow yourself several hours for wandering up and down **Skoufa, Tsakalof, Kanari** and **Pindarou** streets. When your shopping bags begin to weigh you down, stop in at **Bibliothiki** (No. 18A, Kolonaki Square), a chic café, and a great place to observe the passing parade.

Foodstuffs & Spirits

The most convenient place to buy Greek sweets and spirits as gifts or souvenirs is on your way out of the country at **Eleftherios Venizelos International Airport**, where the shops are no longer precisely 'duty free', but the prices are very reasonable.

However, there are three shops located near Syntagma Square where you can browse for comestibles to tide you over on your visit. **Matsouka** (3 Karageorgi Servias Street, tel: 210 325-2054) is open virtually around the clock, offering fine spirits and wines, dried fruits and nuts and foodstuffs from all over Greece, and chocolates, sweets and biscuits of every sort. The place must be seen to be believed.

Aristokratikon (9 Karageorgi Servias Street, tel: 210 322-0546), nearby, is an old Athenian confectioner *par excellence*. Fine homemade candies – and chocolate truffles galore – are the speciality in this tiny shop. Another good place for the sweet-toothed is **Karavan: Authentic Sweets of the East** (tel: 210 364-1540), at 11 Voukourestiou Street, up a pedestrianised street lined with other interesting shops. It specialises in the filo-honey-and-nut sweets that characterise Greek and Turkish cuisine: *baklavá, kadaífi, galactoboúreko*, etc. (They even offer a 'Diet Baklava', surely 'the cubic zirconium of Greek confections'?)

EATING OUT

If you come to love Athens, it will proba-bly happen late on a summer's night at an outdoor Plaka taverna, surrounded by warm-hearted strangers and mellowed by *retsína*. Enjoying Greek cuisine requires an initial leap of faith: you'll find yourself eating the head of the *barboúni* (red mullet), because your Greek waiter assures you it's the best part of the fish; dipping your *bakaliáro* (fried cod), in *skordalia* (puréed garlic sauce), and winding *hórta* (wild greens), smothered in lemon juice and olive oil, around a scepti-cal fork. Go for it. The way to Athens' heart is through its kitchen door.

The deluxe hotels, especially the Athens Hilton and the Ledra Marriott, have some ex-cellent restaurants, but it's in the humble neighbourhoods of Athens that serious eat-ing occurs, so walk there. You'll soon build up an appetite.

Dining in Greece is a specialised affair: one drinks one's *métrio* (medium-sweet Greek coffee) at a *kafeneíon*; one orders starters, *mezédes*, and *oúzo*, beer or *retsína* at a *mezédopoleíon*; one eats as the Greeks do at a taverna, the Greek word for, roughly, bistro; one dines at an *estiatórion*, or

Europeanised restaurant; and one consumes one's *baklavá* or profiterole, at a *zacharo-plasteíon*, or pâtisserie.

One may even bolt down fast food at a *fastfoodáthiko*. The best of these are any members of the homegrown Goody's (after the Greek family name Goudis) chain, where the service and salad bar are good.

What to Eat

Greek food is healthy and tasty. However, there are two surprises for visitors not used to eating Greek dishes; firstly, the food is usually served lukewarm or cold (piping hot food is not considered good for you), and, secondly, a large amount of olive oil used in its preparation. The first is easy to adjust to, but if you find you are having problems with the second, you can try – even though you may elicit some looks of amazement – ask-ing for your food *horís ládi* ('without oil').

If you are vegetarian, you may get bored of *fasoláda* (a stew or soup of haricot beans), *hórta* (greens) and *horiátiki saláta* ('Greek' salad). On the plus side, these dishes are al-most always available, and if you eat fish, then your choice is considerably increased. Other good options include: *kolokithákia/melitzánes tiganités* (fried courgette/aubergine slices), *gígantes* (stewed broad beans), *tyrópitta/spanakópitta* (cheese/spinach pie), *bámies* (okra), *domátes/piperi-és yemistés* (stuffed tomatoes/peppers) and *patátes tiganités/sto foúrno* (fried or oven cooked potatoes).

Meat-eaters have a wide choice of grilled or baked dishes: Greek sausages *(loukánika)* can be particularly good, often containing spices such as caraway; *kokorétsi* (lamb of-fal wound with intestines) is, for all its de-scription, delicious; meatballs *(soutzoukákia/keftédes)* are also a good choice; and don't forget the two classic baked dishes *mous-saká* (minced meat with aubergine) and *pastítsio* (minced meat and macaroni).

Fish in Greece is good but quite expen-sive (the Mediterranean is being fished out). Red mullet and whitebait/smelt *(marídes/atherína)* are the most common types.

In the following listing, based on a three-course meal for two with house wine, € = less than €60, €€ = €60–100, €€€ = €100–160, €€€€ = over €160.

Left: a ring-side seat

Coffee, Sweets & More

Caffé Thanos
2 Evaggelistrias Street, Mitropoleos Square
Tel: 210 322-6681
Open all day, this corner café serves coffees, croissants, quiche, sandwiches, juices, ice cream, etc. Outdoor heaters in winter. €

Doris
30 Praxitelous Street
Klathmonos Square/Agora
Tel: 210 323-2671
Famous for its doughnuts, *loukoumades*, Doris is open all day for Greek specialities as well. Open 7.30am–6.30pm, closed Sun. €

Metropol
1 Pandrossou & Mitropoleos Square
Tel: 210 321-1980/210 322-0197
On the traffic-free square by the cathedral, this is a pleasant oasis all year round. Try the Oriental sweets, or order breakfast. €

Neon
3 Mitropoleos Street, Syntagma Square
Tel: 210 324-6873
Open 7am–midnight.
1 Dorou Street, Omonia Square
Tel: 210 522-9284
Open 8am–11pm.
This cafeteria-style, fast-Greek-food-eatery, with its two convenient locations, serves up coffees, juices, snacks, traditional entrees, pastas and omelettes, and more, in a bright, setting on Syntagma, and a funky, United-Nations-style-smokers'-den on Omonia. €

Yellow Caffe
9 Karageorgi Servias and Voulis streets, Syntagma
Tel: 210 331-9029
This attractive little corner coffee shop is not the place for non-smokers, but the coffees, sweets and clientele are great. €

Late Night Eateries

Estiatorio Papandreou
1 Aristogeitonos &Athenas streets (Central Meat Market)
Tel: 210 321-4970
After a night on the town, brave souls come here for a fortifying bowl of *patsás* – a quintessentially Greek soup, made from the cow's hooves and stomach (and the traditional cure for a hangover). This little 'dive' is open round the clock. €

Palia Vouli
9 Athimou Gazi, Stadiou
Tel: 210 331-4773/210 321-1311
A convivial outdoor café in summer, Italian/ French/Greek restaurant all year round, and an intimate piano bar till the early hours. A treat after a day at the National Historical Museum. Open 8am–2.30am. €€

Polis
5 Pesmazoglou Street (above the Stoa Tou Vivliou)
Tel: 210 324-9588
A beautifully situated terrace-top bar-*cum*-restaurant-*cum*-club, nestling among the Supreme Court buildings. Open for lunch as well. €€

Rebetathiko Stoa Athanaton
19 Sofokleos Street & Stoa (Arcade) Athanaton, Central Market
Tel: 210 321-4362
An authentic late, late-night club for aficionados of *rebétika* (see *pages 74*). The true heart and soul (food) of Athens. €€

Mezedopoleia

Avissinia Café
Plateia Avissinias, Monastiraki
Tel: 210 321-7047
Live music, usually accordion, supporting a good variety of Greek dishes. Closed Sun. Can get crowded. €

The Food Company
47 Anagnostopoulou, Kolonaki
Tel: 210 363-0373
Fresh, healthy (not too much oil), largely vegetarian food. Dishes such as lentils with feta and peppers. Open noon–11.30pm. €

Scholarihio Ouzeri Kouklis
14 Tzipodon Street, Plaka
Tel: 210 324-7605
The bargain-basement of *mezédes*, this starters-only spot is best in summer, when the tables spill out onto the pavement. In business since 1935 – with special rates for groups. €

Taki 13
13 Taki Street, Psirri
Tel: 210 325-4707
This attractively refurbished small, old house serves a variety of well-prepared Greek food and has live music. The area of Psirri has become fashionable and becomes 'yuppie-packed' at weekends. Make reservations. €€

Zeidoron
10 Taki & Aghion Anargiron streets, Psirri
Tel: 210 321-5368
Some modern twists to old Hellenic standards here – and a lovely night-time view of the church of 'The Penniless Saints'. €€

Souvladzíthika

Bairaktaris/Sigalas
2 Monastiraki Square
Tel: 210 321-3036
Old-style Greek taverna right on the square. Standard Greek food, unpretentious, good fare, but specialises is *souvlákia* and kebabs. €

Thanasis
67–69 Mitropoleos Street, Monastiraki
Tel: 210 324-4705
For classic gyro-on-a-pita-plus-onions-tomatoes-and-*tzadzíki*, this establishment, and Bairaktaris, located just across the street, are impossible to beat. Open 8am–2am. €€

Tavernas

Bakalarakia
(also known as **Tou Damigou**)
41 Kidathineon Street, Plaka
Tel: 210 322-5084
This basement *taverna* is supported by an ancient marble column and has a reputation for great *retsina*. Try the fried cod with garlic sauce, radishes, herring and *loukániko* (a spicy Greek sausage). Closed late May to Sept; open Mon–Fri, for dinner. €€

Dimokritous
23 Dimokritou and Tsakalof streets, Kolonaki
Tel: 210 361-3588; 361-9293
A spotless, traditional *taverna*. Good food, moderate prices. Try the array of *mezédes*. Open daily, except Sun. Closed Aug. €€

Karavitis
4 Pafsaniou and Arktinou streets, across from the statue of Truman, Pangrati
Tel: 210 721-5155
Mr Linardos' pre-World War II garden *taverna* is open May–Oct. Order grilled meats and *retsína*. The meatballs *(keftédes)* are superb. Guitar music. €€

Kotopoulou ('The Chicken')
3 Kolonaki Square
Tel: 210 360-6725
This little hole-in-the-wall can't be classified as a taverna. All they serve is spit-roasted chicken, French fries, salad, beer and sodas, but they do it very well. €

Philippou
19 Xenokratous Street
Kolonaki
Tel: 210 721-6390
A disarmingly humble ambience disguises this longtime favourite taverna of archeologists and Kolonaki residents. €

Platanos
4 Diogenous Street, near the Tower of the Winds, Plaka
Tel: 210 322-0666
Stifádo, fish and grilled meats are the specialities here. Lovely atmosphere in summer, when tables are placed under the Plane trees. Closed Sun. €€

Above: meal for one

Rodia
44 Aristippou Street, Likavitos
Tel: 210 722-9883
This is a favourite haunt of foreign archae-ologists. The barrel wine is good. Order veal in lemon or oregano sauce, *bourekákia* (cheese croquettes), *dolmádes* (stuffed vine leaves), and a *horiátiki* (Greek salad). Live music Fri and Sat, closed Sun. €€

Strofi
Petro Galli 25, Makriyianni
Tel: 210 921-4130
Classical Greek *taverna* with a wonderful view from the terrace up to the nearby Acropolis to the north. Closed Sun. €€

Xynou
4 Aggelou Geronta Street, Plaka
Tel: 210 322-1065
Founded in 1936, this restaurant has a gen-uine old-Athens ambience. It serves a great lamb fricassé and offers barrel wine and three strolling guitarists. Closed July, Sat and Sun. €€

Greek and Mediterranean Restaurants

Aigli Bistro
Aigli Zappeion, near Syntagma Square
Tel: 210 336-9363/4
Sophisticated Mediterranean cuisine (with a French twist) in a beautiful setting adjacent the Zappeion. Pricey. €€€

Elia
28 Milopotamou Street, Ambelokipi
Tel: 210 691-0100
The tasteful, minimalist décor of this new restaurant complements the thoroughly mod-ern Mediterranean cuisine. Fresh fish and salads, beautifully presented. €€€

Hermion
15 Pandrossou and 7 Mnissikleous streets, in the arcade, Plaka
Tel: 210 324-67285/210 324-7148
www.hermion.gr
This spotless, air-conditioned eatery is a re-liable retreat after you've spent a full morn-ing shopping in Monastiraki. Try their daily lunch specials. Also open, with live music, for dinner. €€

Kafeneio
26 Loukianou Street, Kolonaki
Tel: 210 722-9056
One of the places to book for dinner if you have only a day or so in the city. This 19th-century lookalike features some 40 starters on the superb menu. Order four or five plates to get a true feeling for the country's cui-sine. The restaurant is refined, intimate, and the service a pleasant surprise. See below for details of another branch. Open for lunch, too. Closed Sun. €€€

Kafeneio
1 Epiharmou Street, Plaka
Tel: 210 324-6916
This is a less pricey version of the Kolon-aki branch, with a more limited menu, but it offers a warmhearted, cosy Plaka atmo-sphere. Try the *saganáki* and *keftedákia* meatballs. €€

Mayemenos Avlos (The Magic Flute Restaurant and Patisserie)
4 Amynta Street, Pangrati
Tel: 210 722-3195
In summer, especially, this garden restau-rant, open since 1961, is wonderful. On a recent visit it was enhanced by live guitar music – Corfiot *cantáthes*. The delicious sweets are an additional perk. €€

Orizondes Likavitou
Likavitos Hill
Tel: 210 722-7065
This hill-top restaurant has the most stunning view in town, plus the exquisite, eclectic, seafood-based cuisine of Chef Ioannis Geldis. Very pricey indeed; reserve well ahead. Open for lunch as well. €€€–€€€€

Right: bright lights, warm welcome

Parko Eleftherias

Vassilisis Sophias Park, near
Megaron Moussikis
Tel: 210 722-3784
www.toparko.gr
Located in an idyllic park setting, this restaurant features a fantastic pepper steak and kataifi cheese pie, among the many other delights on the menu. €€€

Ta Kioupia

2 Olympionikon Street, Politeia/Kifissia
Tel: 210 620-0005
A plethora of classic Greek specialities, but the €40 fixed price menu is superb

value for money for the famished. Reservations necessary; Mon–Sat till late; Sun, only lunch. €€

To Kioupi

Kolonaki Square
Tel: 210 361-4033
This basement restaurant offers no frills, but serves good food at low prices. Closed Sun and Aug. €

Vasilenas

72 Eolikou and Vitolion streets, Piraeus
Tel: 210 461-2457
Reserve a table, starve for at least a day and then arrange for a taxi to pick you up afterwards: the *table d'hôte* consists of some 24 courses. Go with friends and allow several hours to savour your meal. Evenings only, closed Sun; closed lunch; no credit cards. €€

International

L'Abreuvoir

51 Xenokratous Street, Kolonaki
Tel: 210 722-9106
Pleasant French restaurant in a wonderful setting beneath mulberry trees. Also open for lunch. €€€

Boschetto

Evangelismos Park, Kolonaki
Tel: 210 721-0893
Chic Italian establishment in a lovely, green garden setting. Great, deep wine list. Open year round; closed Sun. €€€

Eden

12 Lisiou and Mnisikleous streets, Plaka
Tel: 210 324-8858
Athens' leading vegetarian restaurant with a good selection of organic wines. The fresh fruit juices are delicious, and it has a no smoking section. Closed Tues. Open for lunch as well. €€

Karavi Restaurant/Bar

Ninth Floor, Sofitel Athens Airport
Tel: 210 354-4968
Sophisticated French cuisine and an incredible view, plus over 150 Greek and French wines to choose from. Reservations recommended. €€€

Pil Poul (O Kyrios)

Apostolou Pavlou and Poulopoulou streets, Thisseio
Tel: 210 342-3665
From the red carpet gracing the entrance to all the fine details of this old private house looking up at the Acropolis, this place is plush. The food is also of a very high quality and the service excellent. The house speciality is venison served with chestnuts. Closed Sun. €€€–€€€€

Ratka

30 Haritos Street, Kolonaki
Tel: 210 729-0746
For years this split-level bar has been frequented by the city's fashionable people. The food is of very high quality, but definitely not Greek. Crowded after 10pm, so make reservations. Closed in summer, and Sun; Sat open only for lunch. €€

Above: the end of another good lunch

Hotel Restaurants

Usually, travellers try to avoid dining where they lay their weary heads, but some of Athens' hotel restaurants are too good to miss. **The Athens Hilton** (46 Vasilissis Sophias Avenue, tel: 210 725-0201) has three fine dining establishments to choose from. **The Galaxy Bar**, on the rooftop, combines a fabulous view of the city with fusion cuisine and cocktails; **The Byzantine**, off the lobby, serves an all-you-can-eat brunch; and **The Mythos** promises refined Mediterranean dining.

Other good hotel restaurants include **Café Zoe** at the Athenaeum Inter-Continental (89–93 Syngrou Avenue, tel: 210 920-6655), which features fine buffet dining and a vast array of *oúzos*; and the **Kona Kai**, the Hotel Ledra Marriott's higly recommended Polynesian restaurant (115 Syngrou Avenue, tel: 210 930-0000).

Fish Restaurants

Jimmy and The Fish
46 Akti Koumoundourou, Mikrolimano, Piraeus
Tel: 210 412-4417
This is one of the best fish restaurants on the picturesque Mikrolimano harbour. The grilled fish and seafood pastas are recommended. Expensive. €€€

Plous Podilatou
42 Akti Koumoundourou, Mikrolimano, Piraeus
Tel: 210 413-7910; 413-7790
You'll find here a sophisticated take on the theme of Mediterranean seafood. Reservations are recommended at Chef Alvanides' chic eatery. Also open for lunch. €€€

Psaras/Old Taverna of Psara
16 Erechtheos and 12 Erotokritou streets, Plaka
Tel: 210 321-8733
An island atmosphere pervades this perennial Plaka favourite. Fresh fish is the speciality. Live music every evening but Tues; reservations accepted. €€

Bakeries and Street Food, Etc.

Bakeries, which abound aroundSyntagma Square, especially on **Nikis Street**, are where Athenians buy, and eat, breakfast, generally standing up. Try a *karidópitta* (walnut muffin) or grape-must flavoured biscuits, *moustoukoóloura*, or the old standbys, the *tirópitta* (cheese pie), *spanakópitta* (spinach pie) and the *milópitta*, Greece's version of apple pie. **Apollonon** (10 Nikis Street, off Syntagma Square, tel: 210 331-2590) is particularly recommended.

Busy shoppers on Ermou Street should stop at the **Ariston**, at 10 Voulis Street, where the morning queues advertise its delicious cheese pies. On Athens' street corners you will find plenty of other goodies for sale, including *Kouloúpla*, the chewy, sesame-seed crusted 'bracelets' commuters wear to work to eat with their coffee; roasted chestnuts, which scent the air in autumn and winter; various kinds of nuts; coconut sticks; and roasted corn – stop and nibble.

Internet Cafés

The emphasis, in Athens, is on computing, rather than comestibles, at internet cafés, though Arcade *(below)* does provide an unending supply of coffee for users.

Arcade
5 Stadiou Street, Syntagma area
Tel: 210 321-0701
Smokers and non-smokers retreat to separate areas of this quiet webnettery off Syntagma Square. Open daily 9am–10pm; €3 per hour; no credit cards.

Bits and Bytes
78 Akadimias Street, near the University
Tel: 210 330-6590
Take the metro to the Panepistimiou metro station to reach this huge venue (with some 300 PCs). Not much on eats, but the connection rates are low: €2.50 per hour, 9am–midnight; €1.50 per hour, midnight–9am; no credit cards.

Quick Net Café
4 Gladstonos Street, Omonia
Tel: 210 380-3771
Just 30 PCs here, but convenient to the Omonia metro station. Fees: €2.50 per hour; no credit cards.

NIGHTLIFE

On any given evening in the capital, there is such a wealth of scheduled entertainment that a visitor's primary worry will be choosing what to see and where to go.

The visitor's second worry is finding out about concerts, raves, nightclub acts and performances in time to purchase tickets and get to the venues on time, Athenian traffic being what it is.

Unfortunately, the slick little weekly that lists clubs, acts and concerts (along with restaurants, bars, cinema offerings, etc., etc.), *Athinorama*, is published only in Greek (though there is a large, not-so-timely version published in English once during high season), and the Concert Guide section of the *Kathimerini*, sandwiched into the daily *International Herald Tribune*, is woefully incomplete. *The Athens News* also lists concerts and performances, but if you're more interested in catching Greek *rebétika* (blues) at a dive near the main meat and fish market, or finding what's hot this year but wasn't last (and is therefore not in anyone's guidebook), your very best bet is to purchase *Athinorama* at the corner *períptero* (kiosk), and have a chat with the person behind the desk of your hotel.

The concierge at your hotel is probably your single best source of current entertainment information. You should also ask him or her 'how not to offend' at the particular club you choose to visit: ask him/her to call and find out what the cover charge is, how many drinks one is expected to purchase, whether it's more cost-effective to just buy a bottle, how much one should tip and how to get home safely. Forewarned is the word here, as Athens' nightlife – like the after-hours life of any major city – has rules of its own. That said, Athens after dark is a lot of fun.

The 'sections' in the *Níktes tis Pólis* (Nights in the City) chapter of *Athinorama* bear no relation to listings you'll see in other Western capitals. Athens is, at the best of times, a rather Eastern metropolis, with a thin Western veneer: it undulates to a different drummer, and that drummer can sound decidedly Anatolian.

Cultural Entertainment

The **Herod Atticus Theatre**, just under the Acropolis, is the venue for concerts, theatre and ballet, as well as **Athens Festival** performances, June–Sept (tickets available at the Athens Festival Box Office in the arcade – in Greek, *stoá* – at 39 Panepistimiou Street, tel: 210 322-1459; Mon–Fri 8.30am–4pm, Sat 9am–2.30pm; or at the theatre box office: 9am–2pm; tel: 210 323-2771; 201 323-5582).

Performances of traditional Greek dance are staged by the **Dora Stratou Troupe** in its newly refurbished theatre on Philopappou Hill from the last week in May until the end of Sept, Tues–Sat 9.30pm, Sun 8.15pm; tel: 210 324-4395; 210 921-4650.

Another option is spending an evening at Athens' swish new concert hall, the **Mégaron Moussikís**, on Vass. Sophias (tel: 210 728-2333), which holds performances of Greek, Western classical and popular music. Prior to a performance you can mingle with the Athenian beau monde for wine or champagne or enjoy a pre-ordered supper in the Allegro Restaurant (Level 1; open performance nights; tel: 210 728-2150). Tickets are available from the Hall (Mon–Fri 10am–6pm, Sat 10am–2pm, and on performance days Mon–Fri 10am–8.30pm, Sat 10am–2pm and 6–8.30pm; or at the ticket office at 8 Omirou Street: Mon–Fri 10am–4pm; tickets and information, tel: 210 728-2333 or www.megaron.gr).

Athens is also a good place to catch up on your cinema viewing. All foreign-language films in Greece are shown with Greek subtitles. Again, consult *Athinorama* or the newspapers for shows and times.

Fírmes (Red-Hot Dance Clubs)

The *firmes* have much in common with their New York or London cousins. Up-to-date and usually packed, they are not cheap options for a night out. Though the loud music is Greek and the big crowds are Athenian, the very expensive bottle of Johnnie Walker on the table (more than €100 a pop) is not.

As everywhere, what's 'in' among the *fírmes* changes from year to year, but the following are tried and tested venues and, like most of the *fírmes*, on the coast road, quite a long way from the city centre: it is probably easier to get a taxi there. Arrange for return transport ahead of time, as things can get rowdy around the exits at closing time. It is a good idea to ask your hotel to telephone for opening hours and information.

Iera Odos
18–20 Iera Odos, Gazi (Kerameikos)
Tel: 210 342-8272
Drink €20; bottle of wine €100; bottle of whisky €220.

Posidonio
18 Poseidonos Avenue, Elliniko
(on the beach)
Tel: 210 894-1033

Rex
48 Panepistimiou Street, between the University and Omonia
Tel: 210 381-4591
Drinks €15; bottle of wine €105; bottle of whisky €200.
Rex specialises in well-known Greek performers.

Paradósiaka (Greek Music Clubs)

Paradósiaka are quieter, more congenial night spots featuring Greek music without the amplifiers. Recommended venues include:

To Armenaki
209 Pireos Street, Tavros
Tel: 210 347-4716
Bottle of whisky €100.

Kalokerinos
10 Kekropos Street, Plaka
Tel: 210 322-1679
Bottle of whisky €80.

Summer Nightclubs

These are the most stylish nightclubs and involve hot music, dancing and food.

Balux
58 Vasileos Georgiou B, Glyfada
Tel: 210 894-1620

Banana Moon
139 Megalou Alexandrou, Gazi/Kerameikos
Tel: 210 341-1003

De Stil
4 K. Karamanli, Voula (on the beach)
Tel: 210 895-2403

Inoteka
3 Avissinias Square, Monastiraki
Tel: 210 324-6446

Island
Limanakia Vouliagmenis (on the beach)
Tel: 210 965-3563

Rebétika

Rebétika is a whole complex world of meaning – musical, cultural, philosophical – and, in order to understand it, you would probably need to read Gail Holst's *The Road to Rembetika* and/or be an Athenian Greek of a certain age. Which is not to say you can't just go along and listen, appreciatively.

Rebetika was, at first, the music of the Anatolian refugees who arrived in Athens following the great exchange of populations between Greece and Turkey in 1923. They were concentrated in Piraeus and, among the poverty and unemployment, a lively sub-culture emerged, centred on the *tekedes*, or hashish smoking bars.

The distinctive songs, composed by the musicians who frequented the *tekédes*, deal with nostalgic themes of loss, disposssession and smoking hashish. The songs were accompanied by plucked lutes, the *bouzoúki* and *baglamás*. Although its height of popularity had passed by the 1950s, *rebetika* has been influential on a great deal of subsequent Greek popular music, and a number of contemporary artists have re-recorded old *rebétika* songs.

The listing that follows here is a round-up of the most rewarding venues.

Avissinia Café (Abyssinia Café)
7 Kynetou Street, Plateia Avissinias (Abyssinia Square), Monastiraki.
Tel: 210 321-7047 (Call for hours.)

Call in, just for fun, on Sat and Sun, when the Avissinia Café is so packed you have little hope of being served, or of getting a bill afterwards. This is essentially a local venue.

Charama
Skopeftirio Kaisarianis
Tel: 210 766-4869
Drink €15; bottle of whisky €120.
This dead-authentic *rebétika* club is a long way out of the centre, but worth the drive.

Mnisikleous/Mostrou
22 Mnisikleous and Lysiou streets
Tel: 210 322-5337; 322-5558
Open summer and winter; summer terrace has a view of the Acropolis. Top-flight Greek and other entertainers.

Perivoli Tou Ouranou
19 Lisikratous Street, Plaka
Tel: 210 323-5517; 322-2048
Drink €10; bottle of whisky €85; fixed menu €25.

Stoa ton Athanaton
('Arcade of the Deathless Ones')
19 Sofokleos Street & Stoa Athanaton, Central Market (Kentriki Agora).
Tel: 210 321-4362; 321-0342
All the old *rebétists* such as Koulis Skarpelis and Takis Binis performed here; the drinks are pricey but there's no cover charge; order at least a fruit plate, for appearances' sake. Open from 3pm.

Above: the sound of Athens

CALENDAR OF EVENTS

The Greek year is delightfully interspersed by ancient (read 'pagan', lightly costumed in respectability), Orthodox Christian, and ethnic/historical holidays. Two books available in Athens at Compendium Ltd, 28 Nikis Street, will tell you all you need to know about the Greek year and, more particularly, Greek Orthodox Easter, with all its myriad cultural customs: *The Festivals of Greek Easter*, by Carole Papoutsis; and *Living in Greece*, by The American Women's Organisation of Greece.

To appreciate the full impact of how important the Orthodox holy days can be, you really need to get out of Athens. For example, on 21 May, the *Anastenárides* (fire-walkers) in the Thracian village of Kosti celebrate the feast of SS Constantine and Helen by walking barefoot over glowing coals.

In Athens, your new friends Costas and Eleni may invite you round for drinks to celebrate their Nameday, but you won't find any *Anastenárides* in the capital. Namedays are very important in Greece. The Greeks barely note their birthdays in passing, but do entertain visitors lavishly with sweets, nibbles and drinks on the evening of 'their saint's' nameday. If you have an Athenian friend with an imminent nameday, ask if there are festivities scheduled.

It is a good idea to research the Greek year set out below before your visit. If you make a point of entering into the celebrations it will make your Athenian experience so much the richer. Important Orthodox Christian holy days are denoted by an asterisk.

January

1 *St Basil /Santa Claus*. Nameday for Vassilis, Vassiliki, Vasso. National holiday. Yuletide gifts are exchanged and the *vassilópitta* (Yuletide cake, with a coin, for luck, baked in) is ritually cut.

6 *Epiphany**. Nameday for Fani, Fotini, Fotis, Theofanis. National Holiday. Blessing of the waters.

7 *St John the Baptist*. Nameday for Ioanna, Ioannis, Joanna, Yannis.

17 *St Anthony*. Nameday for Andonis, Antonia, Tonia, Tony.

18 *St Athanasios*. Nameday for Thanasis, Thanos.

25 *St Gregory*. Nameday for Grigoris.

30 *Three Hierarchs* (St Basil, St Gregory and St John).

February

2 *Ipapante/Candlemas**: The Presentation of Christ at The Temple.

10 *St Charalambos*. Nameday for Bobbis, Haris, Harikleia.

14 *St Valentine's Day* (this is not a religious holiday).

Moveable:

Apókries/Carnival. The three-week period preceding Orthodox Lent is Greece's Carnival Season. Fancy dress parties, balls and parades are the norm in many Greek towns and cities, notably on the island of Skyros, in Patras and in Thebes. Check *The Athens News* for events scheduled in Athens, but be sure not to miss the revels in Plaka.
Katharí Deftéra/'Clean Monday'. This national holiday marks the first day of Lenten fasting, seven days before Easter. Kites are flown and picknickers feast on special food.
Saturday after Clean Monday. St Theodore. Nameday for Dora, Roula, Roulis, Ted, Theodora, Theodore.

March

25 *Feast of Evangelismos/ the Annunciation of the Virgin Mary**. Nameday for Evan-

Right: for flights of fancy

gelia, Evangelos, Vangeli, Vangelio. Also, Greek Independence Day. National holiday commemorating the beginning of the Greek Revolution against the Ottoman Turks in 1821. Panepistimiou Street is usually a good place to watch the parades in Athens.

April

Moveable:
Greek Orthodox Easter almost always falls in April.
Megáli Evthomátha/Holy Week*. Many Greeks fast this entire week, especially on Good Friday, which resembles a day of national mourning in Greece.
Megáli Paraskeví/Good Friday*. Shops and businesses close, at least until noon. Most Greeks take part in the sombre rites surrounding the *Epitaphio*/Christ's Funeral Bier in their chosen churches.
Megálo Sávvato/Good Saturday*. All Greeks attend church at midnight to celebrate the Resurrection. The priest, holding a lighted candle in the completely darkened church, proclaims: 'Come ye! Partake of the never-setting Light!' Believers crowd forward, lighting their Easter candles from the priest's own, then from one another's. To one another, then, the congregation repeats, 'Christ is risen. In truth, He is risen', red-dyed eggs are cracked one against another, and the fast is broken.

A very special place to observe the midnight services is atop Mount Likavitos at the Chapel of St George. From the hill's vantage point, the entire city appears to go dark just before midnight, and then trails of fireflies – the candle bearers – multiply in their thousands across Athens.

After services, Athenian housewives return home to cook for the noon feast. Visitors will find ample and representative spreads at all the major hotels in town, including the Athens Hilton and the Ledra Marriott. However, you would need to make reservations in advance.

Páskha/Easter*. This most important day of the Greek year is celebrated with feasting on roast lamb, getting together with friends and family and indulging in joyful recreation.

(All Namedays which fall during the moveable Holy Week are celebrated a week later than usual.)

23 *St George**. Nameday for Georgia, Gogo, Yiorgos.
25 *St Mark**. Nameday for Markos.

May

1 *May Day*. A national holiday and Greece's official toast to spring, marked by workers' parades and excursions to the green countryside, where people

gather flowers and greenery to work into wreaths, which they then hang on their front doors or balconies. There is also much simultaneous feasting at countryside or seaside tavernas.

5 *St Irene.* Nameday for Irini, Rena.
21 *SS Constantine and Helen.* Nameday for Constantina, Costas, Dina, Dino, Elena, Eleni.

June

Moveable:
Pentecosti/Pentecost/Whit Sunday Celebrated seven weeks after Easter.
Whit Monday National holiday

29 *SS Peter and Paul.* Nameday for Paola, Pavlos, Petros.
30 *Twelve Apostles.* Nameday for Apostolina, Apostolos, Tolis.

July

20 *Prophet Ilias.* Nameday for Ilias.
25 *St Ann.* Nameday for Anna.
26 *St Paraskevi.* Nameday for Paraskevas, Paraskevi, Vicky, Vivi.
27 *St Panteleimon.* Nameday for Pantelis.

August

1 Beginning of the *Fast of the Virgin Mary.*
6 *Transfiguration of Christ*.* Nameday for Sotiria, Sotiris.
15 *Dormition/Assumption of the Virgin Mary.** National holiday and day of the great pilgrimage to the Church of St Mary the Evangelistria on the island of Tinos, where the icon of the Virgin is venerated for it power to work miracles. Nameday for Maria, Mary, Panos, Panayiota, Panayiotis.

September

8 *Nativity of the Theotokos*.*
14 *Elevation of the Holy Cross** (day of fasting). Nameday for Stavroula, Stavros, Roula.
15 *Wisdom, Love and Hope.* Nameday for Agapi, Elpitha, Sophia.

October

3 *St Dionysios.* Nameday for Denis, Denise.
18 *St Lukas.* Nameday for Lukas.

26 *St Dimitrios.* Nameday for Dimitra, Dimitris, Jimmy, Mimi, Mitsos.
28 *Ohi* ('No') *Day.* National holiday commemorating Metaxas' standing up to Mussolini and the Italian invasion (with his famous 'No!') in 1940.

November

8 *Archangels Gabriel and Michael.* Nameday for Angela, Angelos, Michalis, Michelle, Stamata, Stamatis.
15 The beginning of the *Fast of the Nativity.*
17 *Polytechneion Day.* School holiday and early business closings. Commemorates the sit-in at the Athens Polytechnic which led to the fall of the 1970s dictatorship. Usually marked by a (largely peaceful) march on the American embassy (as the US supported the junta).
21 *Presentation of the Holy Theotokos*.* Nameday for Maria, Mary, Panayiota, Panayiotis. (Note: there are multiple namedays for some saints, and parents specify which saint's day their children will celebrate when they are baptised.)
25 *St Catherine.* Nameday for Ikaterini, Katerina, Katy.
26 *St Stylianos.* Nameday for Stella, Stelios.
30 *St Andrew.* Nameday for Andreas, Andriani.

December

4 *St Barbara.* Nameday for Varvara.
6 *St Nicholas.* Nameday for Nikolaos, Nicoletta, Nikos.
12 *St Spyridon.* Nameday for Spiridoula, Spyros.
15 *St Eleftherios.* Nameday for Eleftheria, Lefteris.
25 *Christmas*.* National holiday. Nameday for Chrissa, Christina, Christos.
26 *St Emmanuel.* National holiday. Nameday for Emannuel, Manolis, Manos.
27 *St Stephen.* Nameday for Stephanos.
31 New Year's Eve

Other Namedays

In addition to the Namedays mentioned above, those for numerous other saints, from Agni to Zoe, are celebrated. Go to an Athenian bookshop or stationer's for an exhaustive list.

Left: the Acropolis makes a splendid stage

Practical *Information*

GETTING THERE

The new Eleftherios Venizelos International Airport (ATH), located in Spata, some 25km (17 miles) to the northeast of the city, is Athens' main point of entry (tel: 210 353-0000, access www.aia.gr, or phone 144 for flight schedules). Unless you're encumbered by a lot of luggage, by far the most convenient way to get between the new airport and the centre is via two express buses: the E95, which runs to and from Syntagma Square (where the metro connects to elsewhere in the city); and the E94, which runs to and from the Ethniki Amyna metro station. Take the E96 if your destination is Piraeus. The E95 and E96 operate on a 24-hour basis; the E94, 5am–11.30pm. Taxis are plentiful at the airport; the departures rank is located between doors 4–1 of the Arrivals entrance. Fares into the city centre average €15–18.

TRAVEL ESSSENTIALS

When to Visit

For most purposes, Athens is best visited off season, either in spring or in autumn (September through mid-October). Those who want to visit the beaches as well as the ruins should schedule visits for June or July, rather than August, which is hot and crowded.

Easter is becoming increasingly popular with foreign visitors. Check with an Orthodox church in your home country, as the dates of Western and Orthodox Easters usually differ. Tourists visiting between October and May should pack a raincoat, preferably with a warm, removable liner.

A dead-of-winter visit featuring skiing at Arachova, the mountain resort near Delphi, or other developing Greek slopes, is another possibility. Contact the Greek National Tourist Organisation in your home country for information on slope conditions (or log on to www.gnto.gr, www.gnto.co.uk or www.greektourism.com).

Visas and Passports

A valid passport, good for at least three months after the period of intended stay in Greece, is required by all except the following visitors: 1) EU nationals in possession of valid, national IDs and funds sufficient for their stay; and 2) visitors carrying valid national IDs from Iceland, Liechtenstein, Malta, Monaco, Norway and Switzerland. Australian, Canadian, Japanese and American holders of a valid passport and a return ticket do not require a visa. Since there are numerous entry restrictions affecting visitors of other nationalities, it is best to contact the consular authorities in your country of origin while planning a trip to Greece. (Note: visitors arriving by charter flight should check with consular authorities before departing: the return portion of their tickets may be invalidated if they leave Greece – say, for Turkey or Cyprus – and return, at any point during their stay.)

Vaccinations

No vaccination certificates are required for arrival in Greece other than for yellow fever, for visitors 6 months and older travelling from an infected area.

Left: journey through time
Right: for forward planning

Money Matters

Greece adopted the euro (€) as its official currency in January 2002, with notes in denominations of €500, 200, 100, 50, 20, 10 and 5; coins in denominations of €1 and €2, and 50, 20, 10, 5, 2 and 1 cent(s). Major credit cards are accepted nearly everywhere, with the exception of petrol stations and tavernas, which rarely accept plastic (although the more expensive restaurants all take cards). All banks will exchange traveller's cheques, but visitors will pay a smaller handling fee (about 2 percent) at National Bank of Greece branches: you will need your passport to exchange traveller's cheques. There is no limit to the amount of foreign currency or euros you can bring into Greece, but declare any amount exceeding €10,000 upon arrival. There are many ATMs in Athens, including the airport, which will accept cash cards. Banks are open Mon–Thur 8.20am–2pm, Fri 8am–1.30pm.

Foreign Exchange

As strikes and public holidays are common in Greece, always carry extra euros on you. After-hours currency desks offer lower rates and charge a higher commission. The National Bank, Commercial Bank, Alpha Bank, Pireos Bank and the General Bank in the city centre all have 24-hour automated exchange machines for changing foreign currency into euros.

Some of the best places at which to exchange currency are listed below:

American Express Travel Related Services: 31 Panepistimiou Street, tel: 210 323-4781/2/3/4. Open Mon–Thur 8am–2pm; Fri 8am–1.30pm. Also at 2 Ermou Street, tel: 210 324-4975. Open Mon–Fri 8.30am–4pm; Sat 8.30am–1.30pm; closed Sun.

Eurochange: 2 Karagiorgi Servias Street, Syntagma, tel: 210 331-2462; 22 Filellinon and Kydathineon streets, Plaka, tel: 210 324-3997; 10 Omonias Street, Omonia Square, tel: 210 523-4816. Open daily 9am–9pm. The amount of commission depends on amount exchanged – approximately 2.5 percent, higher after 3pm and at weekends.

Thomas Cook Travel Services: 4 Karagiorgi Servias Street, tel: 210 322-0005. Open Mon–Fri 8.30am–8pm; Sat 9.30am–4pm; Sun 10am–4pm.

ELTA: You may also exchange money at the ELTA, the Greek National Post Office, located in Syntagma Square at the corner of Mitropoleos Street.

Banks: The following banks are open for currency exchange Mon–Thur 8am–2pm; Fri 8am–1.30pm. Closed Sat and Sun.

Alpha Bank: 6 Filellinon Street, tel: 210 323-8542.

Eurobank: Filellinon and Othonos streets, tel: 210 325-4195.

National Bank of Greece: 2 Karagiorgi Servias Street, tel: 210 322-2730. Also open Mon–Thur 3.30–6.30pm; Fri 3–6.30pm; Sat 9am–1pm.

ATMs

Scattered around Syntagma and throughout Athens are cashpoints (ATMs) at which you can access foreign accounts or get cash advances from your credit card. Most systems are available, including Cirrus, Plus, Visa, Mastercard, Amex, Eurocard, Diner's Club and Citibank.

Buyer Beware: Check with your credit card customer service representative before using your card for a cash advance. Some card companies charge large fees for this service, which can be a nasty surprise upon your return home.

Duty-Free Allowances

Passengers over 18 years of age from EU countries may import, for their personal use, the following: 800 cigarettes, 400 cigaril-

Left: a favourite way of getting around

Seasonal average temperatures in Centigrade (and Fahrenheit):

	JAN–MAR	APR–JUNE
Minimum	6°C (43°F)	11°C (52°F)
Maximum	16°C (61°F)	29°C (84°F)

	JUL–SEPT	OCT–DEC
Minimum	19°C (66°F)	8°C (46°F)
Maximum	32°C (90°F)	23°C (73°F)

los, 200 cigars or 1kg tobacco; 10 litres of alcoholic beverage, or 90 litres of wine and 110 litres of beer; and perfume in any quantity. Residents of non-EU countries may import the following goods obtained duty-free outside the EU: 200 cigarettes or 50 cigars or 250g tobacco; 1 litre of alcoholic beverage (22 percent or greater) or 2 litres alcoholic beverage (22 percent or under), and 2 litres of wine and liqueur; 50g perfume and 250ml *eau de cologne*; plus gifts valued at up to €175 per person. (Note: visitors from Denmark, Finland and Sweden should check with their consular sections before buying large amounts of tobacco and alcohol products to take home: these countries currently impose limits.)

Clothing

The Athenian summer lasts, generally speaking, from May through September, when lightweight clothing in natural fabrics is recommended. Bring comfortable low-heeled shoes for the marble heights, sunblock, sunglasses and a sun hat. Rain gear is a must between October and May, and winter coats are necessary from December through April. It is important to take precautions against the sun in spring and summer – the smog does not keep out the ultra-violet rays.

Those visiting churches should dress conservatively: women should wear skirts and long sleeves and men trousers. For going out in the evening pack something elegant, as the Greeks like to dress up for the occasion.

Electricity

Power supply is 220 volts AC, 50Hz and sockets accept dual round-pronged plugs (not shaver plugs). Americans will need transformers and converter plugs for their appliances; British visitors, only converter plugs.

GETTING ACQUAINTED

Geography
Greece
Population: 10.9 million
Size: 131,957 sq km (81,994 sq miles)
Athens
Population: 3.8 million (though this may be a low estimate)
Size: 427 sq km (265 sq miles)

Climate

Athens' climate is temperate in winter, with frosts and snowfalls few and far between. Winter days can be delightful, with crisp temperatures and clear blue skies, and spring brings green leaves and colour to the city. That said, rainy weather can occur any time between September and April, though the sun shines at some point most days.

Temperatures rise into the 30s Celsius (90s Fahrenheit) as early as May, and July and August can be unbearably hot, if dry, with temperatures peaking into the high 30°s (100°s) and even 40°s (110°s). Combine this heat with smog cover, and you have a prescription for misery.

Air pollution levels are high all year round, and the number of hospitalisations for respiratory problems is increasing in summer.

GETTING AROUND

Maps and Information

For maps of Athens and Greece indicating bus, trolley and train routes and numbers, visit the Hellenic National Tourist Organisation (Ellinikós Organismós Tourismós, or EOT) in the Eleftherios Venizelos Airport Arrivals Hall, tel: 210 354-5101; 210 353-0445; Mon–Sun 8am–10pm; and 7 Tsoha Street, tel: 210 870-7181 (www.gnto.gr, info@gnto.gr). Excellent maps now abound at the capital's better book stores: be sure your map indicates the new metro stations.

Taxis

On entry, ensure that the meter is switched on and registering '1', the 5am–midnight rate, rather than '2', which is the rate between 1 and 5am (fares double between 2 and 4am). Don't worry if you find yourself

joined, en route, by a large cross-section of Athenian society going roughly your way. It is perfectly legal for drivers to pick up as many people as is comfortably possible, and charge them all individually. The tariff regulations are posted on cards in all taxis.

There is a surcharge from airports, seaports, railway stations and bus terminals; passengers may also be charged a small fee for luggage; and the No. 2 tariff applies for journeys outside the city centre. There has been a spate of extreme overcharging by Athenian cab drivers, so be alert to this scam. The flag down fare is currently €0.73; with a minimum fare of €1.47; and an extra airport surcharge of €1.17. (At the time of this writing, a law requiring all taxi drivers to provide their clients with printed receipts for fares is making its way to enactment.)

Radio Dispatched Taxis

Hailing a taxi is a frustrating business in Athens (you may not be picked up if you do not appear to be going in a 'profitable' direction), so it can be better to arrange taxi transport in advance. It may be easiest to have your hotel concierge phone for a taxi. Your hotelier can also provide a list of reliable 'radio dispatched taxis' to call for your journey back.

Buses

City buses are crowded and usually hot, and the routes are a mystery even to long-time residents. However, they are reasonable, with fares currently set at €0.45, or €2.90 for a 24hr ticket. Tickets (valid for trolley buses as well) are sold in books from most OASA kiosks and special booths at bus and metro stations, and at various points around the city. Most services run until midnight.

Separate services run to air and sea ports, and these can be useful *(see page 79 for* airport services). The Green bus 040 runs from Filellinon Street (near Syntagma Square) to Piraeus 24 hours a day every 20 minutes (every hour after 1am). The Orange bus runs from 14 Mavromateon Street, Areos Park, and takes approximately 1½ hours.

Dial 185 between 7am and 9pm for bus and trolley bus information, or tel: 210 883-6076 (www.oasa.gr). Upon embarking, be sure to validate your ticket in the machines located, usually, to the rear of the vehicle. Failure to do so will result in a fine.

Trolley Buses and Trams

Though marginally more comfortable than the regular bus service, the yellow trolley buses are not recommended for short-stay visitors as their routes are a mystery best left to the locals. However, as this book goes to press, a more efficient tram system being introduced for the 2004 Olympics is fast becoming a reality. This new line will provide fast, inexpensive transportation from the Zappeion, and its nearby Fix and Neos Kosmos metro stations, to Neo Faliro, Paleo Faliro, Glyfada, Voula, and other stops along the sea coast, making it much easier for visitors to get to the beaches from the city centre.

Above: leaving Piraeus harbour

Metro

The brand-new Attiki Metro is by far the best way of getting around the city (for information, access www.attikometro.gr), but the areas serviced by the system are limited. It is is clean, fast, regular and efficient, though not air-conditioned in summer. The old metro (green line 1) runs between Piraeus and Kifissia, and connects Piraeus with Monastiraki and Omonia. City centre stops are at Thisseion, Monastiraki, and Omonia.

Red line 2 runs between Sepolia and Dafni, with city centre stops at Stathmos Larisis (the railway station), Panepistimiou (the university), Syntagma, and Akropoli (the Acropolis). Blue line 3 runs between Ethniki Amyna and Syntagma, with useful stops at the Megaro Mousikis (Concert Hall) and Evangelismos (hospital) near the Hilton. These lines will eventually be extended, with blue line 3 running all the way to the new airport at Spata. There is a map of the Metro on the last page of this book.

Tickets are purchased at metro stations. A single ticket costs less than €1 (currently €0.60 or €0.70, depending on the line) and is valid for a journey of any length in one direction. The €2.90 ticket that gives unlimited travel for 24hrs on the metro, bus and trolley bus is good value.

Railway

The Greek railways are a delight if one enjoys travelling for its own sake, but a frustrating experience if getting there quickly is important. Consider travelling first class, which is only slightly more expensive than second, and infinitely more comfortable.

Railway timetables and tickets may be purchased from OSE offices located at 6 Sina Street, tel: 210 529-7313. Athens has two railway stations, one serving the south; the other, the north: southern, Peloponnisos line, 3 Sidirodromon Street, Athens, tel: 210 513-1601; northern, Larisis line, 31 Deligiani Street, Athens, tel: 210 529-7777.

Ferries and Catamarans

Weekly ferry and catamaran schedules are available from the tourist information offices at 7 Tsoha Street, Ambelokipi, tel: 210 870-7000 (www.gnto.gr, info@gnto.gr). Alternatively, buy the *Greek Travel Pages* from Eleftheroudakis at 4 Nikis Street behind Syntagma Square. As with the trains, investigate first (or A) class (with or without a cabin) as an option: in first class, a degree of comfort can be promised that is noticeably lacking in other parts of the ship.

Book ahead through a travel agent or telephone 143 for ferry schedules and then arrive at the port a couple of hours before departure time: ticket agencies are located next to the ships.

Hydrofoil

The Flying Dolphin is more expensive than the ferries and liable to cancellation in high winds. However, they are speedy and provide a pleasant way to travel to the Saronic Gulf islands, especially at the 'sharp end', which is non-smoking, or, on hot days, in the stern, where there is a small deck. Flights are regular, and tickets are available at the port or at Akti Kondyli and 2 Aitolikou, Pireaus (Hellas Flying Dolphins, tel: 210 419-9000; Saronic Dolphins, tel: 210 422-4775/7).

ACCOMMODATION

Hotels

The hotels listed below have been grouped by their EOT (National Tourist Organisation of Greece) classifications, and have been selected for quality, convenience and service rather than price, although a good range is included. (Luxury Class hotels in

Right: Aegina accommodation

Athens, some pricey even by New York or London standards, vary wildly in terms of facilities available for the money.)

Abbreviations indicate: AC–air conditioning; SP–swimming pool; R–in-house Restaurant(s). I also indicate whether a hotel is located near Syntagma Square or in Plaka, the most convenient locations for those using this particular guide. That said, however, if you can afford a hotel with a pool in high season, splurge: at the end of a long, hot day, a dive into cool water is more a necessity than a luxury.

It is not advisable, in any season, to show up in Athens without a hotel reservation. At best, you will be charged the highest rate; at worst, you will find no vacancies.

My own favourite Athenian hotel is the Parthenon, on Makri Street, in Makriyianni. The location – beneath the Acropolis and convenient to the Akropoli metro station – is perfect. High rollers may opt for the plush, nearby Divani Palace Acropolis.

Consider using a travel agent rather than booking independently. My Athens travel agency, All About Travel (12–14 Karagiorgi Servias Street, off Syntagma Square, tel: 210 331-9401/2, fax: 210 331-9404; email: allabout@ath.forthnet.gr; www.all abouttravel.gr) gets me the best deals by far. And don't decide that a De Luxe hotel is beyond your means: travel agents in Athens are given deep discounts by all hotels.

In the following listing, based on rack rates for a double in high season, €€€€ = over €400; €€€ = €300–400; €€ = €200–300; € under €200.

De Luxe Hotels

Andromeda Athens
22 Timoleontos Vassou Street, Mavili Square
Tel: 210 641-5000; 210 643-7302
Fax: 210 646-6361
Really a collection of unique, plush apartments plus a hotel, this complex is located near the Concert Hall and American Embassy and is ideal for those who need such things as in-room fax machines. The in-house Etrusco restaurant is excellent. AC, SP, R. (Nearest metro station: Mégaro Moussikis). €€€€

Athenaeum Inter-Continental
89–93 Syngrou Avenue
Tel: 210 920-6000, Fax: 210 920-6500
www.athens.intercontinental.com
There are Acropolis views from many rooms and suites here, although this ultramodern 'atrium hotel' is a bit too far from the centre for walkers and a little antiseptic in character. AC, SP, R and many in-house shops. €€€€

Athens Hilton
46 Vasilissis Sofias Avenue, Ambelokipi
Tel: 210 728-1000, Fax: 210 7281111
www.athens.hilton.com
This is Athens' best hotel, newly renovated, with excellent, in-house restaurants (the Byzantine restaurant's all-you-can-eat-€30-lunch is a delight) and the famous, rooftop Galaxy Bar, which has panoramic views of the city. AC, SP, R and many in-house shops. (Nearest metro station: Megaro Moussikis.) €€€€

Athens Park
10 Alexandras Avenue
Tel: 210 889-4500, Fax: 210 823-8420
Located next to the Archaeological Museum, the Park is not the most central hotel, but it features a garage and a roof-top pool. AC, SP, R. (Nearest metro station: Victoria.) €€€

Divani Palace Acropolis
19–25 Parthenonos Street, Plaka
Tel: 210 928-0100, 210 921-7031
Fax: 210 921-4993
www.divanis.gr
A member of the Divanis chain, this newly renovated hotel is located just beneath the

Left: follow that sign

Acropolis and features an in-house museum, with a section of the Themistoclean Walls. It is in easy walking distance of the Herod Atticus Theatre, and Athens Festival performances. AC, SP, R. (Nearest metro stations: Akropoli and Syngrou-Fix.) €€

Grande Bretagne

On Syntagma (Constitution) Square
Tel: 210 333-0000, Fax: 210 322-8034
www.grandebretagne.gr

The most famous hotel in Athens, the GB has undergone a head-to-toe renovation and is now a 19th-century showplace, with every possible perk. Drop in for tea, even if you're not staying. AC, SP, R. (Nearest metro station: Syntagma.) €€€€

Kefalari Suites

1 Pentelis & Kolokotroni streets,
Kefalari/Kifissia
Tel: 210 623-3333, Fax: 210 623-3330
www.kefalarisuites.gr

An elegant hotel, good for those wanting to indulge in a spot of swank shopping in this trendy northern suburb – and who don't mind taking the train into the centre. AC. (Nearest metro/train station: Kifissiá.) €€€

Ledra Marriott

113–115 Syngrou Avenue
Tel: 210 930-0000, Fax: 210 935-8603
www.marriott.com

An American-style luxury hotel with great amenities and fine in-house dining. The rooftop pool has breathtaking views of the Acropolis. AC, SP, R. €€€

Margi House

11 Litous Street, Vouliagmeni
Tel: 210 896-2061, Fax: 210 896-0229
www.themargi.gr

Not for inner-city visitors, this film-set gorgeous Vouliagmeni beach hotel (with its world-class restaurant) is 100m from the sea, with all the perks as well. AC, SP, R. €€€

NJV Athens Plaza

2 Vassiliou Georgiou and Stadiou streets,
Syntagma Square
Tel: 210 325-5301/9, Fax: 210 325-5856

A member of the Grecotel chain, this modern, luxury high-rise is located, like the Grande Bretagne, on Constitution Square. Ask for outside rooms on floors 8 and 9, for their Plaka and Acropolis views. AC, SP, R. (Nearest metro station: Syntagma.) €€€€

Pentelikon

66 Deligianni Street, Kefalari/Kifissia
Tel: 210 623-0650, Fax: 210 801-0314

The Pentelikon is located in a leafy northern suburb, but it's a drop-dead gorgeous edifice dating from 1929, and the service is exquisite. AC, SP, R. (Nearest metro/train station: Kifissia.) €€€€

Royal Olympic

28–34 Diakou Street, Makriyianni
Tel: 210 928-8400, Fax: 210 923-3317
www.srs-worldhotels.com

A comfortable hotel opposite the Temple of Olympian Zeus. Most of the hotel has been modernised, and good deals may be available out of season. Front rooms overlook the temple and Mt Likavitos. AC, SP, R. (Nearest metro station: Akropoli.) €€€

St George Lycabettus

2 Kleomenous Street, Likavitos
Tel: 210 729-0711/9, Fax: 210 729-0439
www.sglycabbetus.gr

Between Kolonaki Square and Mt Likavitos, this eyrie is reached by a steep ascent, but it's a delightful hotel in a posh neighbourhood, with views of the Parthenon. Ask for south-facing rooms with a view. AC, SP, R. (Nearest metro station: Evangelismós.) €€

A and B Class

Airotel Alexandros

8 Timoleontos Vassou Street, Ambelokipi
Tel: 210 643-0464, Fax: 210 644-1084
www.airotel-hotels.com

Very near the Megaron Moussikis (Concert Hall) in Ambelokipi, this business travellers' favourite has beautiful suites, and an on-site Byzantine church. AC, R. (Nearest metro station: Megaro Moussikis.) €€

Amalia

10 Amalias Avenue, Makriyianni
Tel: 210 323-7301/9, Fax: 210 323-8792
www.greekhotel.com.amalia/athens

A popular high-rise, convenient for Plaka and Constitution Square. Ask for rooms with views of the National Gardens. AC, R. (Nearest metro station: Syntagma.) €

Best Western Coral
35 Possidonos Avenue, Paleo Faliro
Tel: 210 981-6441, Fax: 210 938-1207
www.coralhotel.gr
Although located 5km (3 miles) from the city centre, this little high-rise hotel is directly on the beach. AC, R. €

Electra
5 Ermou Street, Syntagma Square
Tel: 210 322-3222/6, Fax: 210 322-0310
A favourite with business travellers and right on Syntagma Square, this hotel is not to be confused with the ritzier Electra Palace. The rooms are small for families. (Nearest metro station: Syntagma.) €

Pan
11 Mitropoleos Street, Syntagma Square
Tel: 210 323-7816/8, Fax: 210 323-7819
Located just off Syntagma Square, this is a small, reliable hotel with comfortable rooms. AC. (Nearest metro station: Syntagma.) €

Parthenon
6 Makri Street, Makriyianni
Tel: 210 923-4594/8, Fax: 210 923-5797
Situated beneath the Acropolis in Plaka, this is a friendly, quiet member of the Airotel chain. Its good service, location and reasonable rates are its most attractive perks. AC, SP, R. (Nearest metro station: Akropoli.) €

Plaka
7 Kapnikareas & Mitropoleos streets, Monastiraki
Tel: 210 322-2096/8, Fax: 210 322-2412
www.plakahotel.gr
Centrally located in Monastiraki, this hotel has roof garden views of the Acropolis. Some rooms, too, look up to 'The Rock'. AC, R. (Nearest metro station: Monastiráki.) €

Stanley
1 Odysseus Street, Karaiskaki Square
Tel: 210 524-1611/18
Fax: 210 524-4611
Good value for money, this hotel has a pool and is next to a metro station, but a hike from Plaka and Syntagma Square. AC, SP, R. (Nearest metro station: Metaxourghío.) €

Titania
52 Panepistimiou Avenue
Tel: 210 332-6200, Fax: 210 330-0700
www.titania.gr
Has lots of facilities for the money, plus a roof-top piano bar, and the Olive Garden Restaurant, with views of the Acropolis. AC, SP, R. (Nearest metro station: Omonia.) €

C Class
Achilleas
21 Lekka Street, Syntagma Square
Tel: 210 323-3197, Fax: 210 322-2412
www.achilleashotel.gr
Situated very near Syntagma Square, recently renovated and with a garage. AC. (Nearest metro station: Syntagma.) €

Adrian
74 Adrianou Street, Plaka
Tel: 210 322-1553, Fax: 210 325-0454
Tiny hotel, really guest house, in the heart of Plaka: views of the Acropolis from the roof garden. Ask for the larger rooms. AC. (Nearest metro station: Monastiraki.) €

Astor
16 Karageorgi Servias Street, Syntagma Square
Tel: 210 335-1000, Fax: 210 325-5115
A favourite of international groups, this hotel is off Syntagma Square. Newly renovated. Some rooms have Acropolis views. AC, R. (Nearest metro station: Syntagma.) €

Above: flying the Greek flag

Athens Cypria
5 Diomeias Street, Syntagma Square
Tel: 210 323-8034, Fax: 210 324-8792
A modest, high-rise hotel just off Syntagma Square. It is quiet, with good service and an adjacent cafe. Great for families. AC. (Nearest metro station: Syntagma.) €

Lilia
131 Zeas Street, Passalimani, Piraeus
Tel: 210 417-9108, Fax: 210 411-4311
If you need to spend a night in Piraeus and want free transfers to the port), this modest, reliable hotel suits nicely. AC. €

Youth Hostel
Youth Hostel
16 Victor Hugo Street
Tel: 210 523-2049, Fax: 210 523-2049
www.interland.gr/athenshostel
This is the only Greek youth hostel certified by the International Youth Hostel Federation. Contact the Greek Youth Hostels Association at tel: 210 751-9530, fax: 210 751-0616 for a list of the hostels they recognise/recommend. Budget.

HOURS & HOLIDAYS

Business Hours
A complicated affair at the best of times, Greek shop opening hours vary depending on the time of year and the type of business. The government is attempting to make Greece more 'European' by abolishing the siesta period. Since hours change seasonally, the best bet is to consult the Useful Information section of the *Kathimerini* insert in the daily *International Herald Tribune.*

Here are the current opening times:
Supermarkets: Mon–Fri 8am–8pm, Sat,7.30am–6pm.
Department Stores: Mon–Fri 9am–8pm, Sat 9am–6pm.
Other Shops: Mon, Wed, Sat 9am–3pm, Tues, Thur, Fri 9am–2pm and 5–8pm.
Tourist Orientated Shops: In season, these will open early, and close very late.

It is best to go shopping in the morning, at around 9am, when everything is sure to be open.

Public Holidays

New Year's/St Basil's (Vassilis') Day:	1 January
Epiphany:	6 January
Ash (Clean) Monday:	moveable
Independence Day/ Feast of the Annunciation:	25 March
Labour Day:	1 May
Good Friday:	moveable
Easter Sunday:	moveable
Easter Monday:	moveable
Assumption/Dormition of the Virgin:	15 August
'Ohi' Day:	28 October
Christmas Day:	25 December
Boxing Day/Dormition of Virgin:	26 December

HEALTH AND EMERGENCIES

Hygiene
Athens' tap water is safe to drink, if occasionally in short supply. Bottled water, both still and fizzy, is readily available (Sáriza, Soroutí and Loutráki are good choices). Choose glass bottles over plastic in summer.

The high levels of pollution in the air, as well as the number of pesticides used in agriculture, mean that you should wash or peel fruit and vegetables before eating. It is also sensible to avoid buying foods that are on open display close to a busy road.

Pharmacies/Chemists
Pharmaceuticals are produced to international standards, and a rotational system is used to ensure that a pharmacy is open somewhere in your part of the city at all times of the day and night. Regular pharmacy hours are 8am–2.30pm Mon–Wed; 8am–2pm Tues, Thur and Fri. All but 'Duty Roster' pharmacies close Saturday and Sunday. Dial 107 for the pharmacy roster in Greek, or check the cards posted in pharmacy windows for the address nearest you (Again, *Kathimerini* has a daily section on Duty Pharmacies in Athens and Piraeus, complete with opening hours.)

Most pharmacists in the city centre speak English, and Greek pharmacists are usually helpful in assisting visitors with treating common minor ailments such as diarrhoea, colds and sunburn.

Health Emergencies

Many Greek hospitals are quickly improving, and horror stories of tourists left alone in wards without adequate nursing care or even food are becoming a thing of the past. However, be sure your travel insurance covers repatriation if necessary.

If you do fall ill in Athens, seek out a reputable doctor through your hotel or embassy. The British, American and other embassies can supply a list of general practitioners and specialists, including dentists, upon request. 24-hour SOS Doctor, tel: 1016.
First Aid and Ambulance, tel: 166.
Poison Centre, tel: 210 779-3777.

Hospitals

The best private hospital and the children's hospitals are located in the neighbourhoods of Ambelokipi and Maroussi, north of the Hilton, and are listed below.

A complete list of the city's public hospitals may be obtained by phoning the Tourist Police on 171. (If you are outside Athens dial 210-171.)

Igeia Hospital (private), 4 Erythro Stavro and Kifissias streets, Maroussi, tel: 210 686-7000.

Children's Hospitals (public): Agia Sofia General Children's Hospital, 3 Thivon and Mikrasasias streets, tel: 210 746-7000. Aglaia Kyriakou Children's Hospital, Thivon and Livadias streets, tel: 210 777-5610.

Safety and Crime

As in all capital cities, poverty, dispossession and lack of opportunities lead people into petty street crime. Although Athens is safer than many cities of comparable size, be sensible and keep an eye on your belongings, and avoid unlit and threatening looking streets at night.

Police Emergencies

In Athens, the police emergency number is 100. The Tourist Police number is 171. Coastguard Patrol is 108.

COMMUNICATION AND NEWS

Telecommunications

Most hotels have telephones, telex and fax and many have internet/email facilities, and there are card phone booths all over town (though they are not always operational). Cards for various euro amounts are sold at most kiosks. If you do not have access to these facilities, head for the OTE offices at 15 Stadiou Street, open 9am–10pm Mon–Sat, and 9am–8am Sun; or on Omonia Square, open 24 hours a day seven days a week.

Dialling internationally is reasonably straightforward. The international access code from Greece is 00. After this, dial the relevant country code:

Australia (61); Canada (1); Germany (49); Italy (39); The Netherlands (31); Spain (34); United Kingdom (44); United States (1).

If you're using a US phone credit card, dial the company's access number: AT&T, tel: 00-800-1311; MCI, tel: 00-800-1211; Sprint, tel: 00-800-1411.

Postal Services

The main post office on Syntagma Square is your best bet for posting everything but packages. They have boxes and reinforced bags for sale at the Express counter at the far end, where you can also send faxes, and the staff are generally friendly and English speaking. (The Express counter is only for fast mailing to the US, or other far-flung locations. For Express mail to European destinations, go to any of the other counters marked 'All Services'.) Packages must be sent from the post office at 60 Mitropoleos Street, but this service is quite expensive in Greece. At both post offices, you must take a number and wait your turn to be served.

Above: periodically profuse *períptero*

Print Media

The many kiosks *(períptera)* throughout the city generally receive British newspapers either late the same night (in Omonia Square) or the next day. There is a reliable home-grown newspaper now half a century old, *The Athens News*, a professional weekly covering Greek and international news, arts, finance and current events. You can access the newspaper on the internet at this address: www.athensnews.gr. Leading the English-language magazines is the glossy *Odyssey*, with quality features on politics, the arts, and wide-ranging topics of general interest. *Greece's Weekly* concentrates on business and finance and is sound in both areas.

The International Herald Tribune includes a translated insert of the Greek daily, *Kathimerini*, which is especially useful for up-to-the-minute information on ferry departures, duty pharmacies and hospitals, and 'radio taxis', as well as the city's erratic shop opening hours.

USEFUL INFORMATION

Airlines

The following listings include straightforward addresses and contact numbers for the larger international carriers, plus contact information for the domestic carriers Olympic Airways and the award-winning Aegean Airlines (the latter, my own preferred carrier for domestic travel). Note: Air carrier and embassy and consulate phone numbers and contact addresses change often in Athens. The monthly publication, *Greek Travel Pages*, which your hotelier will have at her/his reception desk, is the most timely source for this sort of information.

Aegean Airlines
572 Vouliagmenis Avenue, Argyroupolis. Tel: 080 111-20000; airport Tel: 210 353-4294/0101.

Air France
18 Vouliagmenis Avenue, Glyfada. Tel: 210 960-1100; airport Tel: 210 353-0380.

Alitalia
577 Vouliagmenis Avenue, Argyroupolis. Tel: 210 998-8890/8895; airport Tel: 210 353-4284/5.

British Airways
1 Themistokleous Street, Glyfada. Tel: 210 890-6666; airport Tel: 210 353-0453.

Delta
4 Othonos Street, Athens. Tel: 00800 4412 9506; airport Tel: 210 353-0116.

KLM
41 Vouliagmenis and Londou, Glyfada. Tel: 210 911-0000; airport Tel: 210 353-3436; 210 353-1295/6.

Olympic Airways
96–100 Syngrou Avenue. Tel: 210 926-9111; 210 966-6666; 210 969-9111; airport Tel: 210 353-0000.

Swiss International Airlines
5th km Spata-Loutsa Avenue, Spata. Tel: 210 353-7400; 210 353-7500; airport Tel: 210 353-0382/4.

Hellenic Tourist Organisation of Greece (GNTO or EOT)

Australia & New Zealand
51–57 Pitt Street, Sydney, NSW 2000. Tel: (0061 2) 9241 1663–5.
email: hto@pg.com.au

Canada
91 Scollard Street, 2nd Floor, Toronto, Ontario M5R 1G4. Tel: (416) 968-2220.
email: Grnto.tor@on.aibn.com

United Kingdom & Ireland
4 Conduit Street, London W1S 2DJ, London UK. Tel: (020) 7495-9300.
email: info@gnto.co.uk

United States of America
Olympic Tower, 645 Fifth Avenue, NYC, NY 10022. Tel: (212) 421-5777.
email: gnto@greektourism.com

Embassies and Consulates

Embassies in Athens are open Mon–Fri, usually 8am–2pm.

Australia: 37 Dimitriou Soutsou & 24 A. Tsoha streets. Tel: 210 645-0404.

Austria: 26 Alexandras Avenue. Tel: 210 825-7230; 210 825-7240.

Belgium: 3 Sekeri Street. Tel: 210 361-7886/7; 210 360-0314/5.

Canada: 4 Gennadiou Street. Tel: 210 727-3400.

Denmark: 11 Vasilissis Sophias Avenue. Tel: 010 360-8315/6.

Finland: 1 Eratosthenous Street. Tel: 210 751-4966; 210 701-0444.

France: 7 Vasilissis Sophias Avenue. Tel: 210 339-1000.

Germany: 3 Karaoli and Dimitriou streets. Tel: 210 728-5111.

Ireland: 7 Vasileos Konstantinou Avenue. Tel: 210 723-2771/2; 210 723-8645.

Italy: 2 Sekeri Street. Tel: 210 361-7260-3; 210 361-7273/4.

Netherlands: 5 Vasiliou Konstantinou Avenue. Tel: 210 725-4900.

Norway: 23 Vasilissis Sophias Avenue. Tel: 210 724-6173.

Portugal: 23 Vasilissis Sophias Avenue. Tel: 210 723-6784.

Spain: 21 Dionysiou Aeropagitou. Tel: 210 921-3123.

Sweden: 7 Vassileos Konstantinou Avenue. Tel: 210 726-6100.

Switzerland: 2 Iassiou Street. Tel: 210 723-0364/5; 210 724-9208.

Turkey: 8 Vassileos Georgiou Street. Tel: 210 726-3000.

United Kingdom: 1 Ploutarhou Street. Tel: 210 727-2600.

United States of America: 91 Vasilissis Sophias Avenue. Tel: 210 721-2951-9.

THE GREEK LANGUAGE

Greek is a phonetic language. There are some combinations of vowels and consonants which customarily stand for certain sounds, and some slight pronunciation changes determined by what letter follows but, generally, sounds are pronounced as they are written, without additions or omissions.

Thus, learning the phonetic values of the Greek alphabet, and then reading, say, street signs out loud, is an excellent way to start getting the feel of the language.

Most Athenians have some knowledge of English, and most Greeks are delighted to find a visitor making stabs at speaking Greek. (Unlike Parisians, the Greeks do not ridicule you for making mistakes: they themselves have a hard time with Greek spelling and the complicated Greek grammar.) Whatever you can accomplish, guide book in hand, will be rewarded.

In addition to pronouncing each letter, you should remember that stress plays an important role in Modern Greek. When you learn a Greek word, learn where the stress falls at the same time. Each Greek word has a single main stress (marked in the following vocabulary list with an accent).

Greek is an inflected language as well, and noun and adjective endings change according to gender, number and case. Case endings, the rules governing them, and the conjugation of Greek verbs are, unfortunately, beyond the scope of a travel guide book.

The Greek Alphabet

Cap.	l.c.	Value	Name
Α	α	a in ant	alfa
Β	β	v in visa	vita
Γ	γ		ghama
		gh before consonants and a, o and oo; y before e, as in year	
Δ	δ	th in then	thelta
Ε	ε	e in let	epsilon
Ζ	ζ	z in zebra	zita
Η	η	e in keep	ita
Θ	θ	th in theory	thita
Ι	ι	e in keep	yota
Κ	κ	k in king	kapa
Λ	λ	l in million	lamda
Μ	μ	m in mouse	mi
Ν	ν	n in no	ni
Ξ	ξ	ks in jacks	ksi
Ο	ο	o in oh	omikron
Π	π	p in pebble	pi
Ρ	ρ	r in raisin	ro
Σ	σ	s in sun	sigma
Τ	τ	t in tin	taf
Ε	ε	e in keep	ipsilon
Φ	φ	f in favour	fi
Χ	χ	ch in loch	hi
Ψ	ψ	ps in copse	psi
Ω	ω	o in oh	omega

Diphthongs

Type	Value
αι	e in let
αυ	av or af, in avert or after
ει	e in keep
ευ	ev or ef
οι	e in keep
ου	oo in poor

practical information

Double consonants

μπ   b at beginnings of words;
     mb in the middle of words
ντ   d at beginnings of words;
     nd in the middle of words
τζ   dz as in adze
γγ, γκ gh at the beginnings of words;
     ng in the middle of words

Vocabulary

Note: In the following listing words have been broken into syllables, the stressed syllable marked by an accent. Pronounce e as in pet; a as in father; i as in keep; o as in oh.

Numbers

one *é-na* (neuter)/*é-nas* (masc.)/*mí-a* (fem.)
two *thí-o*
three *trí-a* (neuter)/*tris* (masc. and fem.)
four *tés-se-ra*
five *pén-de*
six *ék-si*
seven *ep-tá*
eight *ok-tó*
nine *e-né-a*
ten *thé-ka*
eleven *én-the-ka*
twelve *thó-the-ka*
thirteen *the-ka-trí-a/the-ka-trís*
fourteen *the-ka-té-se-ra*
etc. until twenty
twenty *í-ko-si*
twenty-one *í-ko-si é-na* (neuter and masc.)/
í-ko-si mí-a (fem.)
thirty *tri-án-da*
forty *sa-rán-da*
fifty *pe-nín-da*
sixty *ek-sín-da*
seventy *ev-tho-mín-da*
eighty *og-thón-da*
ninety *e-ne-nín-da*
one hundred *e-ka-tó*
one hundred and fifty *e-ka-to-pe-nín-da*
two hundred *thi-a-kó-si-a* (neuter)
three hundred *tri-a-kó-si-a* (neuter)
four hundred *te-tra-kó-si-a* (neuter)
one thousand *hí-lia* (neuter)

Days of the Week

Monday *Thef-té-ra*
Tuesday *Trí-ti*
Wednesday *Te-tár-ti*
Thursday *Pém-pti*

Friday *Pa-ras-ke-ví*
Saturday *Sá-va-to*
Sunday *Ki-ri-a-kí*
yesterday *kthes*
today *sí-me-ra*
tomorrow *á-vri-o*
day after tomorrow *meth-á-vri-o*

Greetings

Hello *yá sas* (plural/polite)/*yá sou* (sing./familiar) *ya* (abbreviated)
Good day *ká-li mé-ra*
Good evening *ká-li spé-ra*
Good night *káli ník-ta*
Bon voyage *ka-ló tak-sí-thi*
Welcome *ká-los íl-tha-te*
Good luck *ka-lí tí-hi*
How are you? *Ti ká-ne-te?* (plural/polite)/
Ti ká-nis? (singular/familiar)
fine (in response) *ka-lá*
so so (in response) *ét-si két-si*
pleased to meet you *há-ri-ka*

Getting Around

yes *ne*
no *ó-hi*
okay *en dák-si*
thank you *ef-ha-ris-tó*
excuse me *sig-nó-mi*
it doesn't matter *then bi-rá-zi*
it's nothing *tí-po-ta*
certainly/polite yes *má-li-sta*

May I..? *Bó-ro na..?*
When? *Pó-te?*
Where is..? *Pou í-n-e..?*
Do you speak English? *Mi-lá-te ta an-gli-ká?*

Right: transliteration is helpful

Do you understand? *Ka-ta-la-vé-ne-te?*
What time is it? *Ti ó-ra í-ne?* What time
will it leave? *Ti ó-ra tha fí-gi?*
I don't *then* (plus verb)
I want *thé-lo*
I have *é-ho*
here/there *e-thó/e-kí*
near/far *kon-dá/ma-kri-á*
small/large *mi-kró/me-gá-lo*
quickly *grí-go-ra*
slowly *ar-gá*
good/bad *ka-ló/ka-kó*
warm/cold *zes-tó/krí-o*
bus *le-o-for-í-on*
tram *tró-li*
boat *ka-rá-vi, va-pó-ri*
bike/moped *po-thí-la-to/mo-to-po-thí-la-to*
ticket *i-si-tí-ri-o*
road/street *thró-mos/o-thós*
beach *pa-ra-lí-a*
sea *thá-la-sa*
church *e-kli-sí-a*
ancient ruin *ar-hé-a*
centre *kén-tro*
square *pla-tí-a*
airport *aér-o-po-rí-o*

Hotels
hotel *kse-no-tho-hí-o*
Do you have a room? *É-hye-te é-na tho-má-ti-o?*
bed *kre-vá-ti*
shower with hot water *douz me zes-tó ne-ró*
key *kli-thí*
entrance *í-so-thos*
exit *ék-so-thos*
toilet *toua-lé-ta*
women's *yi-ne-kón*
men's *án-dron*

Shopping
store *ma-ga-zí*
kiosk *pe-ríp-te-ro*
open/shut *a-nik-tó/klis-tó*
post office *ta-ki-thro-mí-o*
stamp *gra-ma-tó-simo*
letter *grá-ma*
envelope *fá-ke-lo*
telephone *ti-lé-fo-no*
bank *trá-pe-za*
marketplace *a-go-rá*
Have you..? *É-hye-te..?*

Is there..? *É-hi..?*
How much does it cost? *Pó-so ká-ni?*
It's (too) expensive *Í-ne (po-lí) a-kri-vó*
How much? *Pó-so?*
How many? *Pó-sa?*

Emergencies
dentist *o-don-tí-ya-trós*
doctor *ya-trós*
Help! *Vo-í-thi-a*
hospital *no-so-ko-mí-o*
pharmacy/chemist *far-ma-kí-o*
police *as-ti-no-mí-a*
station *stath-mós*

FURTHER READING

Athens has several English-language book-sellers. The following is a list of recommended English-language book shops in central Athens.
Compendium Ltd. 28 Nikis Street, tel: 210 322-1248.
Eleftheroudakis International Book Centre, 4 Nikis Street, tel: 210 322-9388. Also a huge branch at 17 Panepistimiou Street, tel: 210 335-8440, with coffee and snack bar on the 6th floor.
Reymoundos International Bookstore, 18 Voukourestiou Street, tel: 210 364-8188.

Recommended Books
Since some of these titles are out of print, or not, perhaps, readily available in your country of origin, I suggest searching for used titles online at www.abebooks.com, or new titles at www.greeceinprint.com.
Beard, Mary: *The Parthenon* (Harvard University Press). Essential for all visitors to the Sacred Rock. Beard's a rarity: an academic who's a page-turner. See her thoughtful review of the saga of the Elgin Marbles.
Boleman-Herring, Elizabeth: *Greek Unorthodox.* (2nd ed., Cosmos/Terzopoulos). Essays, and humour, recounting your Insight Pocket Guide author's eventful sojourn in Athens; and, with photographer Clay Perry: *Vanishing Greece.* (Conran Octopus). Coffee-table picture book documenting a fast-eroding traditional culture.
Bouras, Gillian: *A Foreign Wife;*

Aphrodite and the Others; A Stranger Here; Starting Over (Penguin). Beautiful account about being a stranger in a strange land – married to a Greek, the mother of Greeks, the daughter-in-law of Greeks.

Burn, A.R. *The Penguin History of Greece*. (Penguin, various reprints). A good, single-volume introduction to ancient Greece.

Cahill, Thomas: *Sailing The Wine-Dark Sea: Why The Greeks Matter* (Doubleday). This is Vol. IV of the author's Hinges of History series, a compulsively readable, if sometimes controversial, dash through classical history, and the many gifts (and less benign bequests) of the ancient Greeks.

Clogg, Richard: *A Concise History of Greece* (Cambridge University Press). Clear and lively account of Greece from Byzantine times to 1991, with helpful maps and well-captioned artwork. The best single-volume summary.

Davidson, James: *Courtesans and Fishcakes: The Consuming Passions of Classical Athens* (St Martin's Press). A bit rigorous for beach-reading, but a beautifully conceived exploration of what most made classical eyes glaze over. Chapter titles include: Eating, Drinking, Women and Boys…well, you get the picture.

Holst, Gail: *Road to Rembetika: Songs of Love, Sorrow and Hashish* (Denise Harvey, Athens). An exhaustive and colourful introduction to the Greek blues; complete with translated lyrics of standards, and updated discographies (get the most current edition possible).

Kagan, Donald: *Pericles of Athens and the Birth of Democracy: The Triumph of Vision in Leadership* (Simon and Schuster). In this case, the title says it all. A *tour de force* study of 'the great man' in times tailored for and by him.

Keeley, Edmund: *Inventing Paradise: The Greek Journey, 1937–47* (Northwestern University Press). An affectionate and learned introduction to post-war Greece and Athens' fabled 'Generation of the 1930s', Greek and Philhellene writers alike.

Leigh Fermor, Patrick: *Roumeli: Travels in Northern Greece* and *Mani* (John Murray). Written during the late 1950s and early 1960s, before the advent of mass tourism,

these comprise some of the best compendia of the then already-vanishing customs and relict communities of the mainland, plus some of the most beautiful prose written in the English language.

Levi, Peter: *The Hill of Kronos* (Harvill/HarperCollins). Poet-archaeologist Levi's memoir of Greece, from 1963 through the 1990s, evokes the literal and figurative landscape and monuments of Athens and Attica like no other book, and covers well and with passion the country's 7-year ordeal-by-fascism under the Colonels.

Louis, Diana Farr: *Athens and Beyond: Thirty Day Trips & Weekends* (Athens News). A valuable, locally available compendium of excursions in Attica and the Peloponnese, as well as to Spetses, Andros, Kea, Evia and Tinos.

Pressfield, Steven: *Gates of Fire*, and *Tides of War* (Doubleday). Here we have, first, the Battle of Thermopylae and then Alcibiades and the Peloponnesian War. Brainy beach fiction, and a great introduction to ancient Greece.

Stavroulakis, Nicholas: *Cookbook of the Jews of Greece* (Lycabettus Press). Recipes you can follow interspersed with their relation to the Jewish liturgical year, and an authoritative history of the Greek Jewish community.

Taktsis, Costas: *The Third Wedding* (Red Dust). A novel, but rich with cultural and historical accuracy, of the German occupation of Athens – as experienced by two Greek housewives.

Right: street life

ACKNOWLEDGEMENTS

	Bill Wassman *and*
14, 30B	**Apa Archives**
12	**Ashmolean Museum**
15, 33	**Benaki Museum**
59, 70, 86	**Elizabeth Boleman-Herring**
13	**British Museum**
34,	**Byzantine Museum**
29, 61	**Pierre Couteau**
11, 58B	**John Decopoulos**
74	**Guglielmo Galvin**
49	**Greek Archaeological Service**
36, 63, 64, 68, 69	**Terry Harris**
76	**Lebrecht Collection**
35B	**Museum of Pireus**
48T	**Richard T Nowitz**
25, 44	**Maria Stefosi**
40B	**Janos Stekovics**
52	**Topham/AP**
8–9, 22T, 32, 38, 45, 70, 88, 91	**MT Walters & Paul Walters**
2–3, 20, 37, 55, 60, 82	**Phil Wood**
Cover	**Pictor/ImageState**
Back Cover	**Bill Wassman**
Cartography	**Maria Randell**

The author would like especially to thank four Athenians for their help in researching this book: Susan Apostolakis, 'Gourmet-Guru'; Dimitris Gritzalis, 'Athens-By-Night-Maven'; Maria Loumou, 'Researcher Extraordinaire'; and Vassily Loumos, 'Macintosh Rescuer and Peripatetic City Centre Denizen'. *Sas efcharisto, paidia!*

INDEX